Access to History

General Editor: Keith Rand(

D1647149

The Catholic and Counter Reformations

Keith Randell

Hodder & Stoughton

LONDON SYDNEY AUCKLAND TORONTO

The cover illustration shows a portrait of Pope Paul III by Titian (Courtesy Scala)

This book is also available in the Access to A-Level History series published by Hodder & Stoughton.

Other titles in the series:

Luther and the German Reformation 1517–55
Keith Randell   ISBN 0 340 51808 1

John Calvin and the Later Reformation
Keith Randell   ISBN 0 340 52940 7

From Revolt to Independence: The Netherlands 1550–1650
Martyn Rady   ISBN 0 340 51803 0

Spain: Rise and Decline 1474–1643
Jill Kilsby   ISBN 0 340 51807 3

British Library Cataloguing in Publication Data
Randell, Keith
    The Catholic and Counter Reformations.
    1. Spain. Christian Church. Counter-reformation
    I. Title II. Series
    274.6

    ISBN 0 340 53495 8

First published 1990

© 1990 Keith Randell

Typeset by Wearside Tradespools, Fulwell, Sunderland
Printed in Great Britain for the educational publishing division of Hodder and Stoughton Ltd, Mill Road, Dunton Green, Sevenoaks, Kent by Page Brothers Ltd, Norwich

Contents

Preface

This series is intended to provide a concise and easily accessible guide to a range of historical topics and periods, both for the general reader and the student.

For the history student, study guides at the end of each chapter provide diagrammatic summaries of the key points, advice on note taking and advice on handling both essay and source-based questions. To assist with understanding, a * is inserted at various points in the text where a break for a re-read and note making is recommended.

For both general readers and students who wish to pursue their understanding and study of the topic further, a brief selection of suggestions for further reading is included at the end of the book.

Acknowledgements

The publishers would like to thank the following for their permission to reproduce copyright illustrations:

Reproduced by courtesy of Scala, cover and page 106; The British Library, pages 34, 87.

CHAPTER 1

Introduction: The Catholic and Counter Reformations

The term 'Counter Reformation' was invented in Germany in the late eighteenth century. However, it was not in general use among historians internationally until about 1850. It has been in regular use ever since. In German the term was a single word, *Gegenreformationen*, with a plural meaning. It would be translated most correctly as 'Counter-Reformations'. It was first employed to describe the events that took place in a large number of separate German communities in the seventeenth century, when a district which had become Protestant in the previous century was reconverted, often forcibly, to Catholicism. Gradually it came to be used to describe what was claimed to be a general movement. It was argued that the Catholic Church had mounted a coherent, military-style campaign to regain its lost territories, and that the campaign had achieved considerable success.

This concept of the Catholic Church waging a war against its Christian enemies has shaped most historians' thinking about the religious history of the period from 1550 to 1650 for more than 100 years. It has led many of them to concentrate their attention on the political dimension of events. The Wars of Religion, the international dealings of the Papacy, and the division of Western Europe into mutually hostile camps of Catholics and Protestants have been the central issues of concern. The sequence of events that has generally been assumed to be correct is of a Protestant Reformation provoking a Counter Reformation, as the rulers of the Catholic Church realised, somewhat belatedly, that they must either fight or be destroyed. The picture painted has been one of a largely political movement that was a reaction to the actions of Luther, Calvin and their supporters. One French historian captured the spirit of this interpretation by creating the new label of 'religious counter-revolution' for it.

This view of the Counter Reformation as being reactive (a response to the actions of others) rather than pro-active (an independent initiative) is still to be found in a number of textbooks. However, over the past 50 years this interpretation has increasingly been rejected by historians who specialise in the topic. This has particularly been the case with Catholic historians. They have tended to resist viewing this period in the history of their Church as primarily a reaction to Protestantism. They have been keen to stress the ways in which the changes that took place were caused by a general resurgence of spiritual well-being within the Catholic Church. They are happier using the term 'Catholic Reformation' to describe what happened. Some have attempted to establish the phrase 'Catholic Restoration' as the most appropriate label, but they have not been successful.

As so often happens with differing general interpretations of historical 'movements', it has been impossible for one side or the other in the debate on the nature of the Catholic or Counter Reformations to establish the absolute correctness of its view. There is so much evidence that supports the arguments of each side that it would be unreasonable to reject either interpretation out of hand. In addition, there is so much evidence that is missing, either because it has been destroyed, or as yet awaits discovery, or never existed in written form, that uncertainties are bound to remain. To compound the historians' difficulties, the topic is so vast that no one researcher could possibly study all the available evidence, even if an entire lifetime were to be devoted to the enterprise. It covers thousands of named individuals, and millions who are now anonymous, in many countries over a period of more than a century. The significant evidence is housed in a multitude of different archives, and is written in at least a dozen different languages. There has, therefore, been no single historian who has been able to establish himself or herself as *the* expert in the field, whose lead others would be willing to follow.

However, two people have come close to occupying this position. One is Hubert Jedin, a German historian who was at his most influential in the two decades after the Second World War. His international reputation remains high. He is thought of as the person who has known most about the Catholic Church in the Early Modern period. But even he was unable to encompass the whole topic. His major work was an investigation of the political role of the Papacy, focusing especially on the Council of Trent. He devoted relatively little attention to the spiritual dimension of the subject. As a result, his influence has naturally tended to add weight to the arguments of those who see the Counter Reformation as primarily a reaction to Protestantism. This approach has been most widespread in Germany, where, unsurprisingly, historians have tended to be brought up to view the topic with a national perspective. It is events in Germany that best fit the traditional interpretation of the Counter Reformation as a reaction to the rise of Protestantism.

The second outstanding 'expert' is the French historian, Jean Delumeau. Writing in the late 1960s and early 1970s, he argued strongly for a radical revision of the way in which the topic is perceived. He rejected the essentially political, Counter Reformation approach of many of his predecessors, including Jedin, and championed its replacement by an approach that concentrated on the spiritual dimension. He maintained that the history of the Catholic Church could best be understood by emphasising the study of the changing beliefs and behaviours of ordinary church members and, while he did not ignore the actions of leading figures, he minimised their importance. His argument was that the essential change brought about by both the

Protestant and Catholic Reformations was the 'christianisation' of the Church. By this he meant the replacement of the largely mechanistic, spiritually poverty-stricken religious practices – which he saw as characterising the Middle Ages – by a vibrant strain of religion based on faith and commitment and shared in by the population in general. He also argued against the traditional view on time-scales. He freely admitted that the Catholic Reformation was of significant importance in the sixteenth century, but argued (largely using French evidence) that it was at its height in the late seventeenth and early eighteenth centuries. Those working on the topic in British universities, including John Bossy, the leading British historian to specialise in the subject, tend to exhibit considerable sympathy for Delumeau's stress on the practice of religion by the 'common man' as opposed to the activities of the political and religious élites – although Bossy himself has effectively challenged Delumeau's representation of medieval Christianity as almost devoid of spirituality. It is our understanding of the changing significance of religion in the lives of ordinary people that is most likely to be increased by the researches currently taking place.

Nevertheless, the research that has been undertaken in the last 50 years has convinced most writers on the subject that both the concept of the Counter Reformation and the concept of the Catholic Reformation have validity, and are helpful in giving shape to our understanding of western European history in the Early Modern period. There is agreement that it would be a retrograde step to turn back the clock 200 years to the time when writers on the subject saw no coherence in the events that revolutionised the Catholic Church during the sixteenth century. But it should be remembered that the coherence has no existence outside the minds of historians. The Catholic and Counter Reformations are only real in that they are topics for study. They are labels used to describe events that were to have far-reaching effects on millions of people, but they were not events themselves. And, of course, there is still disagreement over which happenings the labels should be used to describe. For obvious reasons, those who think of the Counter Reformation as a response to Protestantism are not prepared to accept that it could have begun before Martin Luther had won widespread support, which would give a beginning date in the 1520s at the earliest. In contrast, those who wish to stress the self-motivated regeneration of Catholicism tend to look back into the Middle Ages for the origins of the spiritual revival they consider to be the main cause of the Catholic Reformation. But at least there is general agreement – certainly in the English speaking world – that it is permissible to use the two terms virtually interchangeably. Within this volume, therefore, reference to one should always be assumed to include reference to the other.

The second major area of disagreement among historians is over which of the two motivating forces for the resurgence of Catholicism had the greatest effect. Did the Catholic Church reform itself mainly because it needed to do so in order to defend itself against the spread of Protestantism, or mainly because of a widespread increase in the spiritual strength of its leaders and members? Of course, there is no simple answer to this question. Issues of historical causation, especially of general movements, are notoriously difficult to resolve. The best that anyone can do is to form a view, based on the available evidence, but to remember the provisional nature of the judgement – and to be prepared to amend it in the light of further evidence.

The aim of this book is to explore some of the most significant issues relating to the topic so that readers will be in a good position to come to informed provisional judgements of their own.

Making notes on 'Introduction'

Your aim in making notes on this brief introduction to the topic should be to assure yourself that you have identified and understood the main issues. It would be helpful for you to keep these in mind as you read the rest of the book.

Write brief answers to the following questions:

1. What are the implications of the term 'Counter Reformation'?
2. What are the implications of the term 'Catholic Reformation'?
3. What are the remaining main areas of disagreement among historians of the Catholic and Counter Reformations?

Studying the Catholic and Counter Reformations

When you are studying the topic of the Catholic and Counter Reformations as part of an examination course, it is very dangerous to select some issues for study and to reject others. Although there are several 'mainline' or 'key' issues within the topic (such as the Council of Trent and the Jesuits) – which are the most frequently found *foci* for examination questions – it is usual for examiners to set questions that require some understanding of the entire topic. If you were to concentrate all your attention on the most popular issues, there would be a real possibility that you would not be able to answer the particular question that will appear in the examination you are to sit. In fact, to be really safe you ought to regard this topic as one of three interdependent topics, and to study all three. The other two topics centre on the work and influence of Martin Luther and John Calvin, and are dealt with by other books in this series. Examiners are fond of asking questions that demand knowledge of aspects of at least two of the topics.

However, it would be misleading to suggest that each part of this book is of equal importance for a student preparing for an examination. Chapters 4 and 5 probably deserve the closest attention as they deal with the most popular 'key' issues, although Chapter 3, on the role of the Papacy, is only slightly less important. Chapter 2 provides essential background that needs to be understood rather than learned in detail. Chapter 6 attempts to provide something of the 'feel' of the spiritual dimension of the Catholic Reformation, and could even be ignored by those who are very short of time. It has been included in the hope of providing a more rounded appreciation of the topic for readers who aspire to a high grade in an examination, or who are particularly interested in religion. Chapter 7 aims to create links with other sixteenth and early seventeenth century European history topics, and is likely to be useful in broadening your understanding of them, rather than providing an issue for study in its own right. It would be most useful to read this during a period of revision. The same applies to Chapter 8, which aims to pull together the topic in a way that many readers will find demanding.

All students are therefore advised to read the whole of Chapters 2, 3, 4 and 5, but not necessarily to proceed to Chapters 6, 7 and 8 on their first contact with the book.

CHAPTER 2

The Catholic Church in the Early Sixteenth Century

1 The Papacy

When western Europeans of the late Middle Ages referred to Christendom they had in mind those countries which accepted the Pope, the Bishop of Rome, as the head of the Christian community. This church was known as the Catholic Church. It was the only church in Italy, Spain, Portugal, France, Germany, Scandinavia and the British Isles. In Poland it was in competition with the Orthodox Church. This was the second of the major Christian Churches, which had converted the peoples on the eastern fringes of Europe to Christianity through missionary activity from its heartland in the Eastern Roman Empire, centred on Constantinople. Originally there had been only one major Christian Church. It had split into its Catholic and Orthodox branches in the eleventh century, largely as a result of the Pope's insistence that he be recognised by every church as its ultimate leader. This the Eastern Churches had refused to do.

By 1500 there had been several centuries of acceptance of the Pope's religious primacy in all parts of western Europe. However, there had been several major crises caused by disagreements over what this primacy meant in practice. These had normally arisen when a Pope attempted to exert influence or control over matters that had traditionally been seen as issues to be decided locally, either by local churchmen or by the area's lay ruler. Such crises had sometimes resulted in 'schism', with those who objected to the Pope's attempt to extend his power at their expense causing an alternative Pope to be elected. At one time there had even been three Popes vying for recognition as the 'true' leader of the Church. It is a reflection of the seriousness with which most medieval rulers treated religion that all the schisms were temporary, and that compromises were eventually reached which restored the unity of the Church. As a result, the idea of the Pope as the undisputed leader of Christendom was a powerful psychological force in much of Europe. Many people disagreed with the actions of particular Popes, but few were prepared to challenge the status of the Papacy as Europe's most important institution.

The Pope was a secular ruler as well as a religious leader. Ever since the break-up of the Roman Empire in the West in the fifth century, Popes had laid claim to territory in central Italy. Their political fortunes had ebbed and flowed, but by the late Middle Ages the Papal States were generally accepted as being a permanent feature of the political map, occupying the breadth of Italy to the north and west of Rome. For centuries this situation had led to frequent disputes between the Papacy and the Holy Roman Emperor, both of whom had aspired to the political control of northern and central Italy. However, in the years immediately prior to 1500, the conflicts had been between the Papacy and the rulers of France and Spain. The monarchs of both these emerging nation states had attempted to seize large parts of the Italian peninsula. Successive Popes had done their best to frustrate these efforts. The resulting wars had never been conclusive, and the struggle was to continue until 1559. Thus, for a large part of the sixteenth century the Papacy found itself involved, often unwillingly, in the trials of strength between the kings of Spain and the kings of France. The situation was at its most difficult during the reign of Charles of Burgundy, a Habsburg, who was King of Spain as Charles I from 1516 to 1556 and Holy Roman Emperor as Charles V from 1519 to 1556. During this period Spain, its overseas empire, the Netherlands, southern Italy, Milan and the Holy Roman Empire were all in the hands of one man. It was with considerable difficulty that the Popes of the period retained a semblance of political independence. Often the price they paid was high. In 1527 Rome itself was sacked by mutinous imperial troops, and in the following decades fear of a repetition of this outrage led to considerable efforts being made to tailor papal policies to meet Habsburg requirements.

Of course, the Papacy was much more than just the Pope. Its central organisation, the Curia, was based in Rome and provided employment for several hundred people. Besides the Pope, its most important members were the cardinals, who were chosen personally by the Pope and who served for life. Their high status resulted from the fact that those of them who were in Rome at the time elected each new Pope on the death of the existing one. By 1500 it had long been customary for them to elect one of their own number, thus reducing (but not removing) the possibility of being pressurised into choosing a servant of one of the leading political powers of the time. In 1522 Charles V managed to secure the election of Adrian of Utrecht, his ex-tutor, as Pope – but fortunately for the independence of the Papacy, he died in the next year. With this exception, sixteenth century Popes were all the free choice of the body of cardinals.

During the late fifteenth and early sixteenth centuries the Papacy was widely criticised. The nature of the Curia was a major cause of complaint. In earlier times, some attempt had been made to reflect the importance of the various nations within the Church in the pattern of appointment of cardinals. However in the late fifteenth century the number of cardinals gradually increased, with most of the new appointments made to Italians. As a result, the relatively few non-Italians were greatly outnumbered as the number of cardinals rose well above 20. In 1517 the situation was thought by many to be totally out of hand when Leo X created 31 cardinals in one day. This seemed to confirm the widely held suspicion that the Papacy was little more than an Italian club working in its own interests. The fears might have been less well founded had the newly created cardinals exhibited some obvious merit. However, many of them had no greater claim to advancement than that they were the friends and relatives of the Pope. Some were children. Thus it appeared that Popes in the future would generally be members or clients of the leading local families, and that the popularly held view that most Popes regarded all non-Italians as barbarians would continue to be accurate.

* Although there were strong undercurrents of hostility to the Papacy in most Catholic countries, much of the criticism came from Germany (see *Luther and the German Reformation* in this series). Anti-papal feelings ran high there mainly because a large part of the Pope's income came from the Holy Roman Empire. Luther was echoing a long-standing grievance when he accused the Pope of milking Germany dry. Because the Emperor had been unable to wrest effective control of the Church in his lands from the Pope, as the kings of France and Spain had done, it was the Papacy that received the huge payments that leading families in Germany were prepared to make in order to secure appointments to lucrative Church positions. It also received the incomes of posts that the Pope purposely left vacant, and the fines paid by the wealthy who wished to receive dispensation from any of the Church's rules. Particularly rewarding was the Pope's ability to allow the children of the very rich to be appointed to bishoprics, although they were below the legal age. Similar complaints of financial malpractice, although fewer in number, were heard from other countries. Especially resented was the way in which the decisions in legal cases taken to Rome – the highest ecclesiastical court – so frequently seemed to be made in the favour of the party that was prepared to pay the most money. There was a widespread feeling that the Papacy was using its powers so as to secure the highest possible income for itself. The popular conception was of a papal shepherd shearing the sheep that it was meant to protect.

* Many people similarly criticised the attitudes, actions, personalities and characters of the Popes of the period. They were seen to be uniformly unchristian, living lives that scandalised those who believed in imitating the behaviour of Jesus as closely as possible. They were accused, correctly, of committing all seven deadly sins between them. Sexual malpractice was commonplace, and most Popes had children whom they openly acknowledged and promoted within the Church. Their interest in religion was often minimal, and some of them were known openly to mock the most sacred of Catholic practices. They seemed to be most concerned with personal pleasure, the advancement of the interests of their families, and the extension of the political power of the Papacy. The low point was reached with Rodrigo Borgia, who

See Preface for explanation of * symbol.

was Pope as Alexander VI from 1492 to 1503. He was even prepared to arrange a series of murders in order to achieve his ends. But he was merely the worst of a sequence of scandalous Popes. They had no conception of providing spiritual leadership to the Church. Most of the Renaissance Popes appeared to act like typical secular rulers of their age. They were cynical politicians who almost always put their own interests first.

2 The Episcopacy and the Lower Clergy

The Catholic Church was organised as a hierarchy. At its head, of course, was the Pope. As Bishop of Rome, he claimed to be the successor to St Peter, to whom, he also claimed, Jesus had entrusted the leadership of His Church. Hence the Papacy's claim to primacy over all Christian churches. Next in line to the Pope were the primates who were the leading churchmen in each of the traditional 'countries' into which Europe was theoretically divided. Beneath the primates were the other archbishops, (primates were also archbishops), who were responsible for specified geographical areas, known as provinces. Each province was divided into dioceses, and each diocese was under the control of a bishop – the exception being that each archbishop was directly responsible for a diocese as well as exercising general control over his province. Most dioceses were divided into parishes, where 'the care of souls' was entrusted to the lower clergy, the parish priests. The word 'episcopacy' is used to describe the archbishops and bishops.

In 1500 there were about 700 dioceses in the Catholic Church. They varied a great deal in size. In Italy they tended to be small, with almost every town of any importance having its own bishop. The situation was similar, although to a markedly lesser extent, in France. Thus there were 273 Italian and 118 French bishoprics and archbishoprics. Towards the fringes of the Catholic world, especially in Britain and in eastern Germany provinces and dioceses tended to be very large. The whole of England was divided into only two provinces, centred on Canterbury and York. There were 19 dioceses. There were 57 episcopal positions in Spain and Portugal and 65 in the Holy Roman Empire. Where large size coincided with local affluence, as was the case in much of Germany and the Netherlands, archbishops and bishops could expect large incomes. This was in contrast to many of their Italian counterparts who were relatively poor.

The Pope was not the only churchman who was also a secular ruler. Many archbishops and bishops, especially in Germany, were the virtually independent princes of their territories. Three of the seven Electors who chose the Holy Roman Emperors were ecclesiastical princes – the Archbishop-Electors of Mainz, Trier and Cologne. The wealth, as well as the political power and social prestige attached to such positions meant that they were much sought after. Long before

1500 it was customary for them to be purchased for the younger sons of the major German princely families. However, the attractiveness of episcopal office was not merely a German phenomenon. Bishops could rely on a high level of material comfort throughout most of western Europe. This they secured either by way of direct income, or via 'considerations' paid to them in return for favours in legal cases and appointments to lower positions within the Church.

In theory, bishops and archbishops were appointed in a variety of ways. In practice, outside Italy, the major influence was frequently the local prince's. Sometimes he could even nominate the person of his choice, as had become the case in France and Spain by 1523. Often he could recommend to the Pope one person for appointment, and unless there was a serious irregularity – where, for example, the nominee already held a similar position, or was a child – the Pope's agreement was little more than a formality. Where the Pope's agreement was not automatic, it could almost always be bought at a price. The Pope's involvement in many Italian appointments was more direct, and he often chose the successful candidate himself.

In most of Europe the quality of bishops and archbishops tended, therefore, to be a direct reflection of the seriousness with which religion was taken by the secular rulers. In the fifteenth century it was exceptional for rulers to consider spiritual issues when exercising their influence over episcopal appointments. The norm was for posts to be viewed merely as one strand in the complex system of patronage. Thus most bishops were either the younger sons of the baronial families whose support was vital to the ruler, or low-born officials of the state whose continued loyalty was being purchased, or whose good service was being rewarded. It was unusual for them to have received any theological training, or to be capable of carrying out any of the spiritual duties of their office. The notable exception to this trend was the Spain of Ferdinand and Isabella in the late fifteenth century, where many men whose spiritual attributes were well-proven were appointed to the episcopacy (see also page 117). The Papacy also appointed a small number of bishops of high quality, although what was more apparent at the time was the custom of bestowing episcopal office on friends, relatives, cardinals and officers of the state, irrespective of their fitness for such positions.

Because so many bishops and archbishops were, in effect, full-time government officials in Rome or in the capitals of other states, absenteeism was a considerable problem. It seems that constant complaints were being made about bishops who rarely, if ever, set foot in their dioceses. The situation was compounded by the widespread occurrence of pluralism. It was not unusual for the really successful political churchmen to acquire four or more episcopal appointments over a number of years. Some dioceses which were subject to a series of political appointments were without a resident bishop for more than a century. When the bishop *did* live within his diocese the situation was often little better. The criticisms that were made of the Popes of the period were echoed for the majority of their bishops, who were castigated as grasping self-seekers, intent on extracting the maximum financial benefit from their office. In many cases this was necessary in order to re-pay the debts that had been incurred in securing their appointment in the first place. Even those who wished to take their duties seriously were faced with huge obstacles. So many churchmen – ranging from heads of monasteries to canons of cathedrals to parish priests – had been exempted from diocesan control by Popes over the years, that in some dioceses the bishop had little real authority. In the diocese of Lyons, for example, more than 90 per cent of parish priests were outside the archbishop's control.

The depths to which the episcopacy had sunk by 1500 was a cause of great concern to those who wished to see a Church that was spiritually active. They realised that the bishops were the only people well placed to bring about the necessary changes. It was they who could visit each locality to ensure that priests were carrying out their duties effectively. It was they who could make arrangements for priests to be appropriately trained. And it was they who could put pressure on the Papacy not to grant exemptions to individuals who wished to avoid the discipline that the bishops were imposing. It is not surprising, therefore, that many of those who looked to reform the Church from the inside considered that the episcopacy was the key to the problem.

Few contemporaries were in any doubt that determined action would have to be taken by the episcopacy if anything was to be done about the generally deplorable state of the lower clergy. The evidence does not exist that would allow historians to carry out statistical research into the tens of thousands of parish priests who were carrying out pastoral duties in Catholic Europe at any one time. However, the mass of anecdotal information that is available paints a picture of almost unmitigated spiritual disaster. Most of the practising priests were untrained and were largely uneducated. Many were barely able to read or to understand more than a little of the Latin they recited during services. Although they were not allowed to marry, a large minority (probably about a third) lived with women who bore their openly recognised children. They lived lives that were in no sense a good example to their parishioners, from whom they could only be distinguished with difficulty. They were in no position to serve the spiritual needs of their 'flocks'. There were many well educated priests but they were mostly absentees, who collected benefices as sources of income and who appointed ill-paid and ill-qualified part-time substitutes to act for them. It would require radical action over several generations to remedy this situation.

3 The Religious

The condition of the religious (the members of a recognised religious order who lived their lives according to a common rule that had received papal approval) was thought to be almost as bad. In the early Middle Ages when warfare, death and destruction were everyday occurrences in western Europe, it had become increasingly common for both men and women to withdraw from the world into the peace and security of a monastery or convent. Thousands of such 'houses' had come into existence. Over the centuries many of them had become very rich. This was both as a result of bequests made to them by the powerful in an attempt to atone for their sinful lives, and the gifts made to them by the families of new entrants, who increasingly had to buy their way in. By 1500 monasteries owned almost a third of the land in many districts, and a significant proportion of the population lived and worked on their estates.

The high ideals that had inspired the original monastic movement, and which had stimulated numerous subsequent revivals, had largely disappeared by the end of the fifteenth century. The vows of poverty, chastity and obedience taken by monks and nuns were said to have lapsed completely in many houses, and the dedication to a life of prayer and hard work for the greater glory of God was widely believed to have been replaced by gossip, idleness and pleasure-seeking. In many cases the public image was correct, and in most countries the houses that reflected their founders' good intentions were in a very small minority. The residents of the houses were often described as 'parasites' on society. Even greater scandal was created by the large number of aristocratic, and sometimes royal, abbots and abbesses who had been placed in charge of the houses as part of the prevailing general system of patronage. Most of them secured papal permission to be non-resident, and satisfied themselves by drawing large incomes from the estate. Many never visited the institutions of which they were the titular leaders. They frequently left the inmates of the house to live in poverty under the direction of a nominated deputy while they enjoyed all the luxuries that money could buy. Spain was the exception to the rule. Under Ferdinand and Isabella there had been a major programme of monastic reform, and most of the more blatant abuses had been corrected by 1500.

The widespread unpopularity of the monasteries was caused by economic as well as moral factors. Secular rulers who were experiencing a period of rising costs and static incomes tended to look at the wealth of the monasteries with envy. In addition, many of those who contributed to the monastic riches through rents or services were aggrieved that the opulence enjoyed by those who had taken vows of poverty was at their direct expense. It was one thing to finance the relative affluence of the gentry and aristocracy – whom it was generally believed had been appointed by God to their superior social positions – but it was quite another matter to surrender a proportion of hard won crops to those who should have been living in equal poverty. It was not by chance that some of the earliest manifestations of popular support for the Reformation were attacks on monastic houses, or that rulers who accepted the Reformation were generally quick to seize monastic lands.

4 The New Orders

The general criticism of the monasteries was not a new phenomenon in the late fifteenth century. It had been a recurrent theme over the previous 400 years. Sometimes the response to the criticism had been the correction of abuses, as it had recently been in Spain, or the division of the order into those who wished to follow a strict interpretation of the Rule (observants), and those who were content to allow more lenient practices (conventuals). Elsewhere the response had been to found new orders, which attempted to avoid the spiritual malaise that was afflicting many of the older foundations. Hence there had been a proliferation of monastic orders over the centuries. Most had followed the same pattern of initial enthusiasm and vigour, often accompanied by the widespread dissemination of their practices throughout western Europe, and later decline into spiritual laxity and material well-being.

Not all the new orders had been monastic. The essential *raison d'être* of the enclosed monastic community was the twin aim of the worship of God and the purification of the soul. It was generally agreed that the second aim was most easily achieved in an environment free from the temptations of the world. Hence a very limited contact with people outside the community. But many committed Christians considered that this formula lacked at least one vital element – the service of one's fellow men in Christ's name. As a result, a number of new orders had been founded in the second half of the Middle Ages with the prime aim of working *within* society. The members of most of these orders were known as friars, of which the most widespread and influential were the Franciscans, the Dominicans and the Augustinians. Martin Luther was an Augustinian friar.

Initially nearly all friars were mendicant – they had no fixed abode. They spent their time journeying from settlement to settlement, begging for food and shelter as they went. The services they offered were preaching (normally in the open air) and the hearing of confessions. They were particularly welcome in communities where there were either no priests or only inadequate ones. By 1500, however, most friars lived a comfortable settled existence, in well-endowed friaries which were in many ways indistinguishable from monasteries. The main difference was that they tended to be town-based and had greater contact with the community – although often at fairly rarified levels. In particular, many universities were staffed exclusively with friars. Work with the poor and needy was much less common than it had been in earlier centuries.

Historians have disagreed furiously about the spiritual state of the Church in the early sixteenth century. Writers from a Protestant background have tended to stress its ills, as a way of justifying the actions of leaders such as Luther, Zwingli and Calvin in destroying the unity of a Church that was apparently beyond saving. On the other hand, Catholic authors have paid considerable attention to the signs of spiritual rejuvenation that appeared to support the view that responsible reformers, with some patience, would have been able to achieve their ends without endangering the unity of western Christendom. Because the study of the Catholic and Counter Reformations has mostly been undertaken by Catholic writers, it is hardly surprising that considerable prominence has been given to the spiritual movements within the Church which pre-dated or were contemporary with the development of Protestantism. Knowledge of them, and especially of the 'new orders' that emerged in the first decades of the sixteenth century, is essential to an understanding of how the topic has been studied by historians.

a) The Capuchins

Some of the new orders emerged from the old – further examples of the process of rejuvenation by division. The Capuchins were the most influential of these. They grew out of the observant branch of the Franciscans. Their name is a corruption of the Italian word for hermit, and provides evidence of the way in which the early members were viewed by contemporaries. The Capuchins aimed to combine abject poverty and self-denial with dedicated work for the poor and underprivileged. They divided their time between contemplation in their wattle and daub hermitages in remote places, and mixing with the poorest elements of society – preaching to them and tending to their material needs. They purposely turned their backs on academic study, relying on their contemplations for spiritual succour and on others to provide instruction on the detail of the Church's teachings. Their message was one of example. They attempted to illustrate what they believed to be God's love for mankind by their own selflessness towards their fellows. They began as a group of a mere four friends in southern Italy in 1520, but they rapidly attracted new adherents in considerable numbers throughout the peninsula. They secured papal recognition as a new order in 1528, and by 1535 there were over 700 Capuchins, growing to over 2,500 by the middle of the century. As was almost always the case with new orders, the Capuchins encountered considerable opposition from established groups. The observant Franciscans were particularly hostile to them, as many of the early recruits came from their ranks.

But their efforts to secure the suppression of the new order were unsuccessful, although in 1536 they did manage to persuade the Pope to prohibit the Capuchins from accepting ex-Franciscans into membership.

The time of greatest danger for the survival of the Capuchins came in 1542 when their charismatic leader, Bernardino Ochino, decided to flee to Geneva to join the Protestant reformer John Calvin, when it became clear that his enemies were about to secure his arrest on grounds of heresy. Ochino, who was a brilliant and inspirational but unschooled preacher, had fallen into the trap of appearing to favour Protestantism by his appeals to his listeners to rely on faith for their salvation. He had thus laid himself open to the charge that he was encouraging belief in the Lutheran teaching of justification by faith alone. His flight showed that he was not the stuff of which martyrs are made and that he had no confidence in his ability to hold his own with trained theologians. But it did not, as his enemies claimed, show that he had been operating as a clandestine Protestant, attempting to bring about a reformation by underhand methods. The Pope came very close to ordering the suppression of the Capuchins, but their unblemished record of selfless service to others, the claim that Ochino was not typical of those he led, and the public esteem in which the order was held ensured their survival.

At the time of their official foundation in 1528 the Capuchins had been limited to establishing houses in Italy. This was a compromise position aimed at silencing the opposition from existing orders. Such, however, was the reputation that the new order gained for itself that it became increasingly difficult for the opposition to prevent this restriction from being lifted. In 1572 it became permissible for the Capuchins to found houses anywhere. By the early seventeenth century the Capuchins, with their distinctive three-cornered hoods modelled on the one thought to have been worn by their spiritual ancestor, St Francis of Assisi, were a common sight in most parts of Catholic Europe.

Catholic historians have been generous, although relatively unspecific, in their assessment of the contribution made by the Capuchins to the Catholic and Counter Reformations. The frequently repeated view has been that they were second only to the Jesuits (see Chapter 5) in the importance of the contribution they made. Unfortunately, however, no balanced case has ever been presented to justify this claim. At best we have a mass of detailed evidence from a large number of disparate sources. From this it is possible to detect the Capuchins' undoubted influence at some times and in some places, such as in the southern Netherlands and in the courts of many Catholic states (especially France) in the early seventeenth century, but it is very difficult to make any convincing assessment of their overall contribution to the Counter Reformation. It is probable that this lack of an overview has largely been caused by the absence of a coherent and readily accessible body of documentary evidence relating to the Capuchins for historians to study – unlike the Jesuits (see page 78). Historians studying the topic of the Catholic and Counter Reformations from original sources, therefore, have had to construct a picture of the impact of the Capuchins from a large number of isolated references. Nobody has yet undertaken the necessary work to produce a definitive study of the order. Meanwhile, historians continue to find that the standard assessment appears to be substantiated by the evidence they discover *en passant* and tend to repeat the orthodox assessment without scrutinising it too closely. In the process, the student is left with little understanding of the exact nature of the contribution, and certainly with no quantification of it.

There is no doubt that the order made a substantial contribution to the Catholic and Counter Reformations by providing many of the personnel for the detailed diplomatic activity between Catholic states during the first half of the seventeenth century. Apart from that, the most that can be said is that the Capuchins, by the power of their example and by the persuasiveness of their preaching, probably convinced many Catholics of the validity of their faith, and thereby made them less likely to fall victim to Protestant propaganda. They also seem to have contributed significantly to the improvement of that unquantifiable commodity – 'morale'. They restored the confidence of many Catholics in their church as an organisation of which to be proud, and as a potential winner in the struggle with Protestantism. They helped to reverse the popular pereception of the Catholic Church as doomed to be the loser.

b) The Oratories of Divine Love

Many of the new orders of the early sixteenth century were unlike any religious organisations that had previously gained official recognition. Some of them were made up of a mixture of ordained priests (clerks regular) and laymen who shared a common desire both to improve the spiritual quality of their own lives and to engage in 'good works' among the sick and the needy. But as the laymen wished to continue with their own lives as well, their commitment to religious activities was only part-time. They were able to compartmentalise their existence, with time devoted to other responsibilities, such as their families, as well as to the religious group they chose to join. The most famous of these groups were those founded in the larger Italian cities under the name of Oratory of Divine Love. The best known Oratory met in Rome between 1517 and 1527. Among its 50 or so members – all members of the aristocracy – were nearly all of the leading supporters of reform in Rome. The members of all the Oratories committed themselves to meet regularly for contemplation, worship, study and charitable work, but they took no vows and wore no uniform. Belonging to an Oratory was not unlike belonging to some modern-day clubs.

Historians have attributed significance to the Oratories as *indicators* of a religious revival that was taking place in Italy in the early sixteenth century. Because their membership was numbered in tens rather than hundreds or thousands, there has been no suggestion that they were responsible for general changes in Italian religious life. However, it should be noted that it was through involvement with the Oratories that several of the men who were to play a key role in the mid-century reforms consolidated their commitment to religion.

c) The Ursulines

Some organisations similar to the Oratories were composed entirely of lay people. The most famous of these was the Ursuline order, an exclusively female order. They originally formed in 1535 as groups of unmarried women meeting monthly and carrying out works of charity, notably the visiting of the sick and the religious instruction of women in their own homes. It was significant that, as with members of the Oratories, they wore no uniform, took no vows, and continued to live their normal lives. It was also indicative of the Church's discomfort both with organisations that required only a partial commitment and with women as other than passive recipients of religion, that the Ursulines were not left to enjoy their half-and-half existence for long. In 1546 they were required to adopt a standard form of dress, in 1566 it was ordained that they should live communally, and in 1595 they were turned into a traditional enclosed order of nuns with the normal vows of poverty, chastity and obedience. Over the next two centuries the order flourished, especially in France and Italy, and became the main provider of Catholic education for girls. It is to be suspected that it was this later influence and popularity that has led historians of the Catholic Reformation to include the Ursulines in their list of notable new orders of the early sixteenth century. Certainly there has been no suggestion that, at that stage, they amounted to more than an example of the religious re-awakening that was taking place in Italy.

d) The Theatines

Similar status should be accorded to the examples in the third category of novel new orders – those made up exclusively of priests. The most frequently described of these is the order of the Theatines. The Theatines owed their prominence to the fact that membership was restricted to the sons of the nobility, hence giving them automatic élite status, and that their co-founders were two of the outstanding church-men of their generation. Cajetan was that rare being, an outstanding theologian with a saintly disposition. He was a natural choice for the Pope to send to Germany in 1519 in an effort to persuade Martin

Luther to conform to the Church's teachings. He provided the Theatines with spiritual stature. But the driving force for the order was provided by Carafa, a determined man of business for whom compromise was a sign of weakness. His iron will was well displayed during the years 1555–1559 when he occupied the papal throne as Paul IV (see page 32). It was no surprise that the order took its name from the Latin form of one of his bishoprics.

Between them, Cajetan and Carafa were well equipped to steer their order from its foundation in 1521 to its official recognition in 1533. During this time it established for itself an international reputation as a model order of priests who wished to take their vocation seriously, and who wished to combine communal living with dedicated service to the wider community. They set new standards for other priests to follow in that they took their official duties completely seriously, while finding sufficient time to ensure their own continuing spiritual development. However, it seems that the publicity about the Theatines outstripped the reality of their achievements. They were never more than a symbol, an example of what might be achieved. They were indirectly influential in that their prominence helped to establish a new tone for the Church, but their direct contribution was limited by the fact that they remained a small group. They never significantly exceeded the 31 members they had in 1533 at the time of their formal inauguration.

e) Assessment

Histories of the Catholic Reformation have traditionally stressed the importance of the emergence of the new orders in the early sixteenth century. It is tempting to imagine that the prominence accorded to this relatively minor phenomenon has been out of proportion to its actual significance. It is even possible to surmise that in some cases writers have unthinkingly accepted the views of their predecessors and have reproduced earlier judgements without questioning their validity. They may even have fallen into the trap of conferring significance to events because of later developments that were linked to them, but were not directly caused by them. Certainly there has been very little close examination of the exact nature of this significance. Instead there has been a rather cosy acceptance of a prevailing orthodoxy.

However, it would be unwise to dismiss the new orders without attempting to understand the claims that have been made on their behalf. Unfortunately, historians have seldom made these claims explicitly. Normally they have been implied by the events that individual authors have chosen to recount. It is immediately noticeable that the new orders traditionally described were all based in Italy. Yet the major re-birth of enthusiasm and discipline that took place in the Church in Spain a little earlier under the influence of Ferdinand and Isabella and largely under the direction of Cardinal Ximenes has been virtually ignored. This suggests that it is the Italian context of the new orders that provides one explanation of the importance assigned to them by the historians of the Catholic Reformation. These authors seem consciously to have been seeking out evidence of a spiritual re-awakening in the peninsula as a background to the emergence of a reform party in Rome. The Capuchins, the Oratories, the Theatines and the Ursulines, together with the half dozen other groupings that have been described from time to time, have been used to provide the context for the stirring events that followed. This does not, of course, automatically mean that they had any real significance in their own right. In particular, many historians have used the new orders as an introductory background to the development of the Society of Jesus (the Jesuits), which clearly *was* an organisation of the greatest significance (see Chapter 4). Yet there can be no suggestion that there was any causal relationship between the Italian orders and the Society of Jesus, which was conceived in Spain and germinated in France. The only direct connection appears to be the somewhat spurious one that the Jesuits were another new order sanctioned by the Pope.

It therefore seems reasonable to suggest that the contention that the new orders (apart from the Jesuits) were of major historical significance remains largely unsubstantiated. In particular, there is a need to clarify the traditional claims made on behalf of the Capuchins, which, although seemingly realistic, are remarkably vague. Equally, it is important that the *effects* of the new orders are examined more rigorously before a full assessment of their significance is attempted. In the meantime, however, there is no difficulty in justifying the claim that the emergence of the new orders, along with the reforms taking place in Spain, proves that the Catholic Church in the early sixteenth century contained much that was positive, rather than being all negative, as has been regularly suggested by Protestant writers during the past 400 years. It was in many ways a spiritually dynamic institution whose leaders generally did it scant justice. The contention that the emergence of the new orders marks the beginning of a new development that typified the reformed Catholic Church is also convincing. If withdrawal from the world, as practised by monks and nuns, was the hallmark of the medieval Church, then the charitable works carried out by many of the new orders was typical of the Counter Reformation Church.

The Catholic Reformation was in part an awakening of the Church's leadership to the forces of regeneration that had become active beneath them. Martin Luther was by no means the only person to take action to restore the Church to its supposed former glory. But unfortunately for the cause of Church unity, the many calls for change were for a long time not taken seriously within the Curia in Rome.

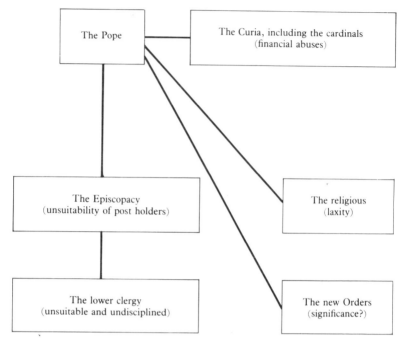

Summary – The Catholic Church in the Early Sixteenth Century

Making notes on 'The Catholic Church in the Early Sixteenth Century'

The aim of this chapter is to provide you with an understanding of three aspects of the Catholic Church: the way in which it was organised in the early sixteenth century, the abuses that existed in it, and the evidence of spiritual regeneration evident in the new orders founded in Italy. Your notes should assist you in answering six questions:

1. What was the structure of the Catholic Church? Your answer need only be brief as this is background information. Perhaps an annotated chart would be suitable.
2. What were the major abuses that were thought to require reform?
3. What was the significance of each abuse to contemporaries?
4. Who was responsible/to blame for each of the abuses? (Questions 2, 3 and 4 could be answered together, in the form of a list with explanations.)
5. What were the distinctive features of the new orders which were founded in Italy in the early sixteenth century?
6. How far do you agree with the significance accorded to the new orders by Catholic historians?

CHAPTER 3

The Reform of the Papacy

1 Background

During the first two decades of the sixteenth century the idea of reform was not even on the Popes' mental agenda. Julius II (1503–13) and Leo X (1513–21) devoted all their energies to other matters. Of most pressing importance was the international political situation. Most Popes through the centuries had been interested in foreign affairs, especially in the relations between the Papacy and the Holy Roman Empire. The two had traditionally been rivals for influence in northern and central Italy, and it had been necessary for each to keep a careful watch on events in order either to take advantage of opportunities as they arose or to avoid being outmanoeuvred by the other. The situation had become immensely complicated towards the end of the fifteenth century. First Spain, in the form of Aragon, had acquired a base in southern Italy – from which attempts could be made to extend influence northwards – and then the French had established a dominant position in most of the peninsula as a result of the invasions of Charles VIII and Louis XII. These developments had undermined the Papacy's position as an international power, and had even seriously endangered its continuation as an independent political unit. The most influential Romans thought that there could hardly be a more pressing problem than this. Therefore it did not seem strange to many contemporaries that Julius II was more of a soldier than a churchman, and that warfare and diplomacy were the centres of his attention as he schemed to play off France, Spain and the Empire against each other, and to make gains for the Papal States at their expense.

In contrast, Leo X was no warrior. He contented himself with diplomacy. His room for manoeuvre was much reduced when the young Charles V added first Spain to his Burgundian inheritance, and was then elected Holy Roman Emperor. In the process, the foreign rivals were reduced from three to two, with the Habsburgs effectively surrounding the Papal States. The best that Leo could achieve was to avoid being swallowed up. At the same time there was the very real possibility that the Ottoman Turks would extend their empire into Italy. Leo expended much of his energy on fruitless attempts to secure support for a crusade against the infidel. In the circumstances, it is hardly surprising that little time could be devoted to dealing with the indiscipline of Martin Luther, an otherwise obscure academic theologian in Saxony.

However, it should not be imagined that Julius II and Leo X were single-minded. There were two other interconnected occupations that consumed a great deal of time and energy. It had become traditional for election to the papal throne to be used as a means of furthering family fortunes. Popes were not isolated individuals. Most of them possessed an extensive circle of family and friends, often including openly acknowledged children. All of these expected to benefit directly from the election of their patron to St Peter's throne. The protection and furtherance of personal interests was a major papal activity. Closely linked to this was the need to retain a dominant position in the political in-fighting that was the main centre of interest within the Curia. A Pope who did not devote enough time to reinforcing his position within the forum of Roman politics soon found himself isolated and effectively powerless. Neither Julius II nor Leo X fell into this trap. As a result both men found themselves fully occupied with activities and concerns that were not essentially religious. They ignored what later generations have identified as their proper duties not because they were particularly wicked men, either by contemporary or modern standards, but because they did not perceive that there were any issues of higher priority than those they tackled, even though they were aware that not everybody agreed with them. They were men of their time, living according to the expectations that had surrounded them from their youth.

★ A long-term change in atmosphere seemed certain in 1522 when Adrian of Utrecht was elected Pope as Adrian VI (sometimes known as Hadrian VI). It was expected that he would concentrate his attention on religious rather than political issues. Not only was he a non-Italian and a stranger to Roman factional politics, he had also been Charles V's tutor and was assumed to be his loyal supporter. It was therefore anticipated that under Adrian the Papacy would meekly accept its reduced status as a scarcely autonomous adjunct to the Empire. To complete the contrast, Adrian was a man who had no personal following to satisfy, and who was genuinely interested in religious matters. He was of a saintly disposition, and, although his election was an indication that the Papacy had at least temporarily succumbed to the power of the Emperor, it seemed probable that a period of papal reform was about to commence. He filled the church-politicians of Rome with horror when he publicly admitted:

1 We know that for many years many abominable things have
   occurred in this Holy See, abuses in spiritual matters, transgressions of the commandments, and finally in everything a change
   for the worse. No wonder that the illness has spread from the
5 head to the members, from the Supreme Pontiffs to the prelates
   below them. All of us (that is, prelates and clergy), each one of us,
   have strayed from our paths; nor for a long time has anyone done
   good . . . we will expend every effort to reform first this Curia,
   whence perhaps all this evil has come, so that, as corruption
10 spread from that place to every lower place, the good health and
   reformation of all may also issue forth. We consider ourselves all

the more bound to attend to this, the more we perceive the entire world longing for such a reformation.

But all the speculation of contemporaries was in vain. Adrian died the next year, after only 18 months in office, and before he had had time to find ways of overcoming the obstructions to reform that were placed in his way by those who surrounded him. He had promised much but had achieved little. The fact that in his final months he reverted to some of

1492–1503	Alexander VI	1555–9	Paul IV
1503	Pius III	1559–65	Pius IV
1503–13	Julius II	1666–72	Pius V
1513–21	Leo X	1572–85	Gregory XIII
1522–3	Adrian VI	1585–90	Sixtus V
1523–34	Clement VII	1590	Urban VII
1534–49	Paul III	1590–1	Gregory XIV
1550–5	Julius III	1591	Innocent IX
1555	Marcellus II	1592–1605	Clement VIII

The Popes of the sixteenth century

the financial abuses he had earlier condemned suggests that even had he lived longer, he might not have been a great reformer in practice. The epitaph on his grave read:

1 Woe! how even a most righteous man's power to act depends on the times in which he happens to live!

* Adrian's successor was Clement VII (1523–34). Clement was Leo X's cousin, and signified a reversion to the old style of political Pope. His interest in reform was very limited, and his weakness of character ensured that the forces of inertia triumphed. He received a dramatic shock in 1527 when his attempts to free the Papacy from the shackles of imperial domination back-fired in horrific fashion. He had thrown in his lot with France, hoping that by so doing a balance of power would be created that he would be able to manipulate to his advantage. Unfortunately for Clement's plans, Charles V was able to neutralise any threat from France by defeating the only army she had in Italy. But he was unable to pay his own forces and they took out their spite on a virtually defenceless Rome. The city was sacked mercilessly. For more than a month 20,000 mutinous troops satisfied their appetites in rape and pillage. No person and no property which attracted their attention was spared. Even nuns were sold from soldier to soldier.

Charles was powerless to stop the tragedy, but he was not displeased that a clear message had been given: active papal opposition to his policy would have dire consequences. However, another message was also received. The Sack of Rome was widely interpreted in Italian church circles as a sign that God was displeased with the way in which His church was being run. Many, including the Pope, who had previously looked upon reform as an interesting possibility for some distant time in the future, now came to accept that changes would have to be introduced as a matter of some urgency. This reversal in the prevailing atmosphere strengthened the position of the small group of cardinals who had been trying for several years to persuade others that reform was an urgent necessity. There was still no great enthusiasm for change among the powerful political élites of Rome, but at least there was a reluctant acceptance that reforms would definitely have to take place at some time. Clement VII was weak. He managed to survive by making vague promises of future action, sometimes with dramatic but unintended effects, as students of English history will know (Henry VIII's attempts to secure a divorce from Catherine of Aragon). By adopting this strategy he avoided making any significant changes, but it was unlikely that a successor would be chosen who was so lukewarm towards reform.

2 Paul III (1534-49)

Alexander Farnese, who was elected Pope as Paul III on Clement VII's death, was a most interesting and complicated man. He defies any simple categorisation. He was in many respects the archetypal old-style political Pope. Yet he displayed a genuine love of religion and the Church and was, on occasions, willing to put the long-term health and welfare of Catholicism before his own and his family's short-term political interests. Although he was very inconsistent, his achievements were considerable. However, his background was unpromising for the cause of reform. He was a member of one of the princely Italian families that for centuries had viewed the Papacy and the Church primarily as sources of power and income, available to be competed for by the political élites of central Italy. He had been made a bishop at the age of 20 and a cardinal five years later. This was not unusual in his circle. Nor was the fact that he showed not the slightest interest in religion. What was unusual was that he experienced a spiritual awakening in later life that led to him being ordained a priest in his fifties. However, his conversion did not make him a totally changed man. He did not lose his interest in selfish worldly matters. Rather, he added religion to his range of enthusiasms.

Alexander Farnese was an old man of 66 when he became Pope as Paul III. It was not unusual for a man to succeed as the head of the Church when he was thought to be within a few years of death. This was designed to ensure that power would not reside in one pair of hands for too long. In Paul's case the strategy was not effective. He was full of energy and vitality when he became Pope and he remained so for 15 years. Despite his good health and expectation of a long life, the new Pope took urgent steps to further the fortunes of his family. Two of his 15-year-old grandsons were immediately created cardinals. It took much longer to resolve the long-running dispute between the Papacy and the Farnese family over extensive lands to which both laid claim. Finally, the ancient duchy of Parma and Piacenza was reconstituted out of the territory of the Papal States, and Paul's disreputable son was installed as its ruler. Few Popes had so shamelessly raided the territorial inheritance that had been entrusted to them.

Yet the unscrupulous self-seeker was also a determined reformer. As might be expected – given the man he was – his motives were complex. In part he was being selfish. There was a danger, although not a very great one, that a failure to reform might lead Charles V to carry out his threat to replace Paul as Pope. There was also the fear that if the Papacy was not reformed other rulers might follow Henry VIII's example in England and establish national churches independent of Rome, leaving Paul with much reduced power and influence. But he was also motivated by a conviction that the correction of abuses and the generation of increased spiritual vigour were desirable as ends in themselves. In addition, he was committed to safeguarding the Papacy's long-term interests by attempting to establish a solid basis of support among Catholic rulers.

Paul gave a clear indication of his intentions when, within months of his election, he appointed six of the most influential supporters of reform in Rome as cardinals. Four of them had been members of the Roman Oratory (see page 16), two of whom – Contarini and Carafa – were men of outstanding quality. Gasparo Contarini (1483–1542) possessed a background that was in some ways similar to Paul III's. He was a Venetian nobleman who had lived the early part of his life largely uninfluenced by religion. At the age of 28 he had experienced a dramatic conversion, and thereafter had made the spiritual health of the Catholic Church his main interest. Although he remained a layman, and continued to serve Venice as an ambassador until he was made a cardinal, he was as committed to reform as any of those whose attachment to the Church was more formal. He was interested in two types of reform. He considered that the doctrines of the Church should be revised in the light of recent scholarship, for although he was in no sense a Lutheran, he could see that some of the Protestants' arguments carried considerable weight and he was not too proud to learn from them. He was also convinced of the need for institutional reform, especially in the way in which the Papacy exercised its powers. He possessed a powerful intellect and a pleasing personality but, unfortunately for his cause, his effectiveness was finally restricted by his lack of worldly wisdom.

Contarini's naivety first became apparent in his actions over the *Consilium de emendenda ecclesia*. A commission was established by Paul III in September 1536 to recommend to him ways in which the Church should be reformed. There were nine members of the commission, under Contarini's leadership. All but one of the members were convinced reformers, and Contarini assumed that the time for radical reform had arrived. The commission worked with great energy and within nine months its report was prepared. Its title was *Consilium de emendenda ecclesia*. It showed the determination of the reformers to place the Church's pastoral responsibilities at the top of the list of priorities. Sweeping institutional changes were proposed. The Papacy was to end its customary selling of exemptions to the wealthy. These exemptions had allowed the young to be ordained, monastic leaders and others to be non-resident, and canon law and the authority of bishops generally to be circumvented by those who could afford to pay (see page 8):

1 There is another abuse which ought not to be in the least tolerated, and by which the whole Christian people is scandalised: it consists in the obstacles which hinder bishops in the government of their flocks, especially in the chastising and correcting of

5 criminals. For, to begin with, wicked men, especially clerics, find
   ways to exempt themselves from the jurisdiction of their ordinar-
   ies [bishops]. And again, if they are not exempt, they forthwith
   fly to Penitentiary or to the Datary [departments in the Curia],
   where they immediately find a way to impunity, and what is
10 worse, in return for cash.

The Papacy was also to abandon the sale of positions within the
Church, which in future were to be awarded solely in the interests of
those who were to be served. Bishops were to be resident in their
dioceses (thus none could be cardinals, whose duty it was to advise the
Pope in Rome) and were to devote their time to training and supervising the priests for whom they were responsible. Past Popes were
criticised for having established and operated a corrupt system:

1 Flatterers have led some Popes to imagine that their will is law;
   that they are the owners of all benefices so that they are free to
   dispose of them as they please without taint of simony. This
   conception is the Trojan horse by means of which numerous
5 abuses have penetrated into the Church. These evils must be
   ruthlessly suppressed. Only such men must be ordained whose
   fitness has been carefully ascertained – in Rome by two or three
   prelates designated for the purpose and elsewhere by the bishop
   of the diocese. Bishoprics and benefices with cure of souls
10 attached must not be granted for the purpose of providing a man
   with a livelihood but in order to secure shepherds for human
   souls. All contrary curial practices must be abolished, such as the
   charging of a benefice with a pension in favour of a third party
   who is not in need but by which the holder of the benefice is
15 robbed, if not of the whole of his proper revenue, at least of a
   great part of it; resignations of bishoprics while their revenues are
   retained, the right of collation to benefices and regresses, since
   these practices make such dioceses practically hereditary; expectatives and reservations as a result of which it often happens
20 that deserving men are excluded or one and the same benefice is
   bestowed on two candidates; the accumulation of several benefices in one hand and the concession of dioceses outside Rome to
   cardinals who as the Pope's official counsellors form his entourage
   and are therefore in no position to discharge their pastoral duties.

Paul III was more politically astute than Contarini. He realised that
to implement the recommendations of the *Consilium* in full or at great
speed would be revolution, not reform, and would create such a storm
of protest from those likely to lose from the changes that it might almost
be as dangerous to the Papacy as the continuation of the abuses. In
addition, the reforms would substantially reduce the papal income, an

eventuality that needed to be planned for. Paul, therefore, decided to approach the recommendations of the *Consilium* with caution. He rapidly accepted them all in principle, but stated that he needed time to consider the most appropriate ways of implementing them. In the meantime, he refused to authorise the report's publication. Contarini was greatly distressed at this turn of events. The report was published without permission in 1538, presumably in an attempt to pressurise Paul into taking action. The result was not as intended. Paul remained unmoved, but the Protestants in Germany were jubilant. Here was a clear confession of the corruption of which the Lutherans had long complained. A Protestant edition of the report, containing an apposite commentary prepared by Martin Luther himself, was widely circulated in northern and central Europe, reinforcing prejudices against the Papacy in the process.

Contarini was essentially an idealist, while Paul III was a realist. Contarini was confident that it would be possible to reach an accommodation with the Lutherans on the basis of an agreed statement of major beliefs. He thought that it would be possible to overcome the mass of mutual hatred and mistrust that had been generated between the two sides by the vitriolic propaganda that had poured from the presses. In particular, he refused to recognise that the Protestants were serious in their rejection of the primacy of the Pope – an issue over which there was no room for compromise, as primacy, like chastity, is indivisible. However, he continued to seek agreement, motivated by a refusal to accept that the divisions within the Church might lead to permanent schism. His belief was that as schism was unacceptable it had to be avoidable. His hopes were shared by Charles V, who could see no other outcome to the Lutheran revolt than a negotiated settlement.

Paul III was sceptical but allowed Contarini to represent him at the Regensburg Colloquy of 1541, which was stated by Charles V to be his last attempt to seek an agreement with the Protestants. Because Contarini's flexibility and desire for a successful outcome were matched by that of Philip Melanchthon, the leading Lutheran delegate, considerable progress was made. But it was not enough. It was impossible to paper over disagreements about issues such as papal supremacy. Even the measure of agreement that was reached was rejected by the absent leaders of the two sides, the Pope and Martin Luther. Certainly with hindsight, and probably with worldly wisdom at the time, it is possible to judge that the venture was doomed to failure. Contarini died a disappointed man in 1542.

Although Paul III had been unwilling to support Contarini when it mattered, he had not been totally inactive. Nor had he satisfied himself with gestures such as the appointment of the reformist cardinals, and the acceptance in principal of the recommendations of the *Consilium de emendenda ecclesia*. He had quietly reduced both the number and the scope of papal exemptions and had ordered that the 80 bishops living in

Rome should leave and take up residence in their dioceses. However, these were minor achievements considering what needed to be done and they were insignificant in comparison with his decision to summon a general church council. This decision, made in 1536, was possibly the most important single action taken by a Pope in the sixteenth century. The direct result of this decision was the first series of sessions of the Council of Trent, which began in 1545. However, it should not be imagined that the nine year hiatus between the summoning and the meeting of the Council was caused by papal delaying tactics. It required considerable tenacity on Paul's part to ensure that the Council met at all. The delay was of others' making. The fact that the Council actually met was greatly to Paul's credit.

* Not all the Catholic supporters of reform in the 1520s and 1530s were of one mind. The large majority, of whom Contarini was a leading example, were 'Christian humanists' who supported the 'new learning' that the Renaissance had brought. They desired both institutional reform and the reform of dogma. They were sympathetic to some of the teachings of the Protestants, especially on the necessity of faith for salvation, but they were committed to the pursuit of reform from inside the Church, rather than by separating from it. In this they were completely opposed to the Protestants, whom they wished to win back to the Church, with compromises if necessary.

If the majority could be termed 'liberal reformers', then the minority might best be described as 'conservative reformers'. Their leading figure was the cardinal Gian Pietro Carafa (later Pope as Paul IV). Their views on institutional reform coincided with those of the liberal reformers, but they were diametrically opposed to them on matters of dogma. They agreed that there needed to be a clear and complete definition of Catholic beliefs, which had not previously existed. However, they advocated a definition based on traditional teachings, ignoring the findings of the humanists, whom they regarded as little better than schismatics. Instead of seeking agreement with the Protestants, they wished to stress the Catholic Church's differences with them, and to confront them rather than to woo them. They believed that the Catholic Church would only be safe once the Protestants and all their sympathisers within the Church had been driven out or destroyed. They were the proponents of a counter reformation. In more modern times they would have been labelled counter-revolutionaries.

During the early years of his pontificate, Paul III was sympathetic to the liberal reformers, as witnessed by the prominence he accorded Contarini. But his sympathies changed at about the time of the Regensburg Colloquy in 1541, when he seems to have fallen largely under Carafa's influence. The reasons for the change are not known, but it seems likely that Paul was finally persuaded that Contarini's tactics were doomed to failure. He was probably also disturbed by the publicity given to the reports of rapidly growing numbers of Lutherans in the cities of northern Italy. It must have seemed to him that what had happened in Germany was about to happen in his native land. He decided to follow Carafa's advice and take decisive action. The advice was to follow the course that had been pursued in Spain when it had faced similar problems more than a decade previously. In Spain a centralised Inquisition had been re-established and had been given overriding powers to investigate all accusations of heresy. In July 1542 a similar organisation was re-established in Rome. It was called the Supreme Sacred Congregation of the Holy Office, and is generally referred to by historians as either the 'Holy Office' or the 'Roman Inquisition'.

The Roman Inquisition was to become the major weapon in the campaign against liberal Catholicism and Protestantism in Italy. Its powers were enormous. In practice, it was able to act against any person, irrespective of status or position, in any Italian state except Venice. Although the hostile writings of generations of Protestant authors have portrayed it as being essentially the equivalent of the secret police in a twentieth century totalitarian state, it is probable that it was no more inhuman (just more efficient) than the secular author- ities of the time. Nevertheless, because the people brought before it – often as a result of anonymous accusations – were considered guilty unless they could prove their innocence and because brutal torture was used as a matter of course on accused and witnesses alike, the Inquisition has justifiably received a bad press in liberal quarters. Conscious efforts were made to ensnare the rich and famous so that the general population would understand that there was no escape from the Inquisition's gaze. Carafa was placed in charge of the new organisation. He was relentless in the pursuit of Protestants and of those suspected of sympathising with their views. Within 20 years the fear of expressing unorthodox views had become an ingrained pattern of behaviour throughout Italy. In the process, and thanks to the earlier work of the Spanish authorities, both peninsulas of southern Europe had been saved for the Catholic cause.

Yet it should not be imagined that Paul III became a cypher in his later years. Powerful as Carafa became, he was not able to persuade Paul that the summoning and holding of a Council was a dangerous adventure and an unnecessary risk. Paul was determined to seek the support and advice of Church representatives from as many lands as possible to the reforms that it was increasingly felt should be made. He resisted all the pressure from Carafa and his supporters to abandon the plans for the Council that was taking so long to come to fruition. The facts that the Council actually met in 1545, that it was in session periodically over the next four years, and that its achievements were significant (see pages 41–6) stand greatly to Paul's credit and indicate that he was a strong and independent-minded leader of the Church.

* Historians have generally been sympathetic to Paul. The prevailing view has been that he is to be forgiven his many faults because they were more than balanced by his positive achievements. This stance is particularly understandable because Paul's most glaring 'sins' were concerned with furthering the interests of his family. The implication has often been that such behaviour should be overlooked as it was the norm of the period for the social class from which he came and as, in any case, it is thought by most people to be a somewhat endearing fault that did no direct harm to anyone. Perhaps it is a comment on contemporary moral values that Paul III's image is of the naughty boy who came good in the end.

However, if Paul's pontificate is judged according to criteria relating to long-term historical significance there is no need for special pleading. His 15 years in power mark the change from the almost exclusively materialist Renaissance Papacy to the spiritually dynamic Counter Reformation Papacy. He consciously committed himself and his successors to a process of reviewing all aspects of the Church's life through the machinery of the Council, knowing that as a result it would be very difficult for reform to be side-stepped in the future. He thereby started a virtually irreversible trend of Catholic reformation, having already given the movement enhanced credibility by appointing its leading members to positions of prominence, and by taking a personal interest in and officially supporting even minor groupings of promise. Thus he gave his patronage to the Ursulines, accorded recognition to the Jesuits, and defended the Capuchins when most of the Catholic hierarchy was against them following the defection of Ochino to Geneva. Even if his own spirituality was sometimes overwhelmed by his materialism, he was able to recognise saintliness in others and to protect and encourage it. Although Paul III was more of a facilitator than an achiever, there is no doubt that he played a significant part in changing the ethos of the central government of the Church – from one in which political and material self-seeking was paramount, to one in which spiritual values predominated.

3 The Consolidation of Reform

However, it should not be imagined that after Paul III there was an unbroken progression from vice to virtue in the Papacy. The pace and direction of change depended almost totally on the personalities and opinions of individual Popes, and these varied considerably. There were periods when the pace of change was so slow that it was virtually undetectable. But there was no back-sliding. Once an abuse was corrected it was not possible for it to be re-introduced. The supporters of reform were too powerful at all levels in the Church for this to be allowed to happen.

The deliberations and decrees of the Council of Trent provided a momentum for reform in the 1550s and 1560 (see Chapter 4). In undramatic fashion during this period, the work of Paul III in correcting the most glaring abuses of papal power was continued. By the end of the 1560s Popes were no longer appointing unsuitable people as bishops. Nor were they allowing wealthy Catholics to purchase exemptions from ecclesiastical discipline by appealing directly to Rome. The decisions that led to this situation were individually unspectacular, but were collectively of great significance. As a result of the changes it was possible for reforming Catholics in the localities, whether they were ecclesiastics or local rulers, to insist that Church discipline was followed, without fearing that their positions would be undermined by contrary decisions emanating from Rome. Thus local initiatives for reform were, in effect, supported from the top, rather than being sabotaged, as so often had been the case in the past.

Several Popes of the second half of the sixteenth century stand out for their contributions to the reform of the Papacy. Carafa was Pope as Paul IV from 1555 to 1559. He was determined that the Papacy should reform itself without the assistance of others. He was, therefore, unwilling to recall the Council of Trent, which remained 'out of session' during his pontificate. In keeping with his justified reputation as an arch-conservative in matters of dogma, he believed in firm discipline rather than persuasion as a method of achieving his ends. He ensured that the Roman Inquisition enjoyed a pre-eminent position in papal politics, continuing the work it had begun in the latter years of Paul III's pontificate. Leading liberal reformers were driven from Rome or imprisoned if they chose to remain. Between 100 and 200 friars (the figures quoted vary) who were living disreputable lives in Rome were rounded up and sent to the galleys from which few would have emerged alive, and even the tolerant authorities of Venice were prevailed upon to surrender notorious heretics so that they could be burned in Rome. In 1559 the *Index* was published, which forbade Catholics to possess or to read an enormous list of books, including the works of liberal Catholics as well as the outpourings of the Protestant propagandists. Paul IV even came close to disbanding the Jesuits (see page 80) because he could not accept their abandonment of traditional collective worship. It was not surprising that most citizens of Rome overlooked Paul's quiet but effective correction of many of the remaining financial abuses of the Curia when they celebrated his death as a release from unfeeling oppression in 1559.

* Pius V (1566–72) seemed in some respects to be a clone of Paul IV. This was perhaps not surprising as he had been the head of the Roman Inquisition during the mid-1550s. But Pius was more than this. Although he, like Paul, waged a moral clean-up campaign in Rome (his major target was the large homosexual community) and dealt harshly with all who were suspected of unorthodox views, he also exhibited spiritual qualities of the highest order. It was claimed that he lived a virtually sin-free life, totally devoid of self-interest. For this he was

subsequently canonised. In keeping with his dislike of pomp and personal status-seeking, he reduced the size of the papal court by 50 per cent to about 500 people. He expected others to make similar sacrifices, persisting in his determination that financial probity should be apparent in the centre and that clerical discipline should be enforced in the localities. In many ways his pontificate marked the high point of the reforming Papacy, not so much for what he did as for what he was. Such purity was far removed from the worldliness of many of his sixteenth century predecessors.

* Pius V and his successor, Gregory XIII (1572–85), continued the reforming tradition that had been initiated by Paul III. They removed what remained of the corruption in the Curia and lent their authority to the implementation of the disciplinary arrangements decreed by the Council of Trent (see page 57). However, it was left to Sixtus V (1585–90) to lead the way in reforming the institutions of the Papacy so as to make its government more effective and efficient. Part of the reason for the slow pace of reform in much of the previous 50 years had been the virtual impossibility on occasions of securing action from the cumbersome and disorganised administrative machinery of the Curia, even when there had been a desire for change from the top. Not only had it been difficult to identify who should take the necessary action, but there had been no way of forcing post holders to act where they disapproved of what was being done.

It had long been known that what was needed was a streamlined series of departments, each with clear-cut responsibilities and chains of command. But no Pope had been able to cut through the 'red tape' of the existing machinery. Sixtus V had the determination and drive to do so. He reorganised the Curia into 15 permanent departments, called congregations, each of which had a discrete area of responsibility, and was led by a small group of cardinals, with specialist advisers as necessary. He accepted the long held view that the number of cardinals should be limited and that they should be capable of carrying out the duties to be assigned to them. He stipulated that there should be no more than 70 cardinals, and that they should be suitably qualified. The work of the congregations was to be supervised by the Pope, although in practice this meant his personal secretary. The personal secretary was normally a trusted close relative of the Pope and the success of any papal administration largely depended on the quality of this post holder. Although the new system was still sometimes at the mercy of uncooperative cardinals, it was a great improvement on what had gone before and, with minor modifications, it served the Papacy well for several centuries.

Sixtus V's reputation as a reforming Pope rests largely on the way in which he reorganised the Curia. But his fame amongst contemporaries was as the Pope who changed the face of Rome. He was a city planner on a grand scale, and although many of his plans did not come to fruition until long after his death, the inspiration had clearly been his. Most typical of his vision was the way in which the quantity of good drinking water available in the city was greatly increased by undertaking engineering works of which the emperors of classical times would have been proud. At last it could be seen that the boundaries of the Dark Ages had been rolled back.

Sixtus V was the last of the great reforming Popes. The practices that

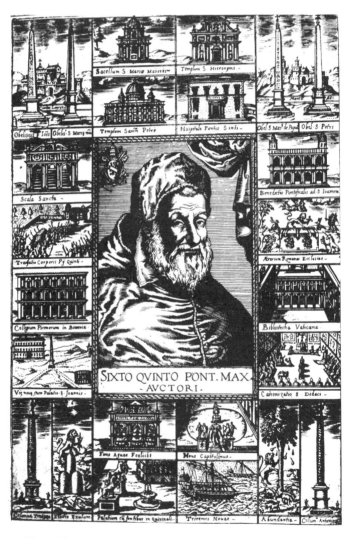

Sixtus V's achievements

had scandalised so much of Christendom at the start of the century had been abandoned, and reasonably fair and efficient government had been instituted. In the process the Papacy had ceased to be a major international force. The ending of corruption had drastically reduced the papal income, especially from outside Italy. No longer could a forward foreign policy be assumed, especially with the costs of warfare escalating so rapidly during the century. From about 1600 onwards the Papacy was increasingly of local Italian importance alone in political affairs. It did, of course, retain a major influence in spiritual matters, but it wielded little real power. The initiative had very much passed to the lay rulers, and it was they who decided whether the religious rivalries generated by the emergence of Protestantism would be exacerbated or would be calmed. Once the Papacy had put its own house in order it was for others to determine the fate of the political counter reformation. This theme is pursued in Chapter 7.

Making notes on 'The Reform of the Papacy'

Protestants demanded the reform of the Church 'in its head and members'. Although this chapter touches on the reform of the Church in broad terms, it concentrates on the steps taken to reform the 'head' – the central organisation of the Church based in Rome and under the Pope's direct control. Your notes should reflect this concentration. You will probably find it most helpful if you structure your notes chronologically, so that you will more readily appreciate the pattern of events through time. Keep one question in mind throughout – 'Why did reform take place at some times and not at others?' The following headings, sub-headings and questions should assist you:

1.   Background.
1.1. What were the priorities of Julius II and Leo X during their reigns?
1.2. Why was so much expected of Adrian VI as a reformer?
1.3. In what sense was the reign of Clement VII a turning point?
2.   Paul III.
2.1. Paul III's reforms.
2.2. The Roman Inquisition.
2.3. Assessment of Paul III's contribution to the reform of the Papacy.
3.   The Consolidation of Reform.
     What contribution to reform was made by:
3.1. Paul IV?
3.2. Pius V?
3.3. Sixtus V?

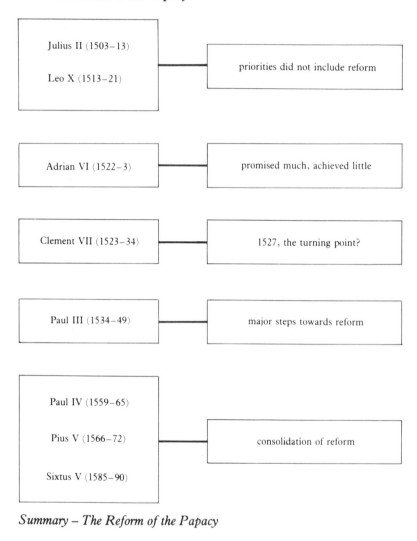

Julius II (1503–13)

Leo X (1513–21)

priorities did not include reform

Adrian VI (1522–3)

promised much, achieved little

Clement VII (1523–34)

1527, the turning point?

Paul III (1534–49)

major steps towards reform

Paul IV (1559–65)

Pius V (1566–72)

Sixtus V (1585–90)

consolidation of reform

Summary – The Reform of the Papacy

Answering essay questions on 'The Reform of the Papacy'

Examiners have been keen to set questions on both 'the reform of the Papacy' and 'the role of the Papacy'. The two are not the same. One is restricted to the changes made in the way in which the Papacy operated as the central government of the Church, while the other requires a consideration of the part played by Popes in all aspects of the Catholic and Counter Reformations. Which is which? Which can be answered from the material in this chapter and which will require you to select evidence from throughout the book?

Questions on 'the reform of the Papacy' almost always demand that you start by identifying *what* was reformed. It is worth having this analysis ready before you enter the examination room. Make a list of the aspects of papal reform that have been discussed in this chapter. You may wish to use a hierarchy of headings and sub-headings. For example, 'financial' could be divided into its component parts.

However, the questions often go on to ask you to comment on the *extent* of the reforms. Sometimes the phrase 'to what extent' signals this requirement, but more often the phrase 'how far' is used. You will remember that the plan for an essay that is essentially about 'extent' should be in two parts. One part will focus on 'thus far' and/or 'in these respects', while the other will explain 'not to this extent' and/or 'not in these respects'. Which part will come first? Which will have more space devoted to it? Consider these questions:

1. 'How far had the Papacy been reformed before the death of Paul III (1549)?'
2. '"The outstanding achievement of the Counter Reformation was the reform of the Papacy." Do you agree?'
3. 'To what extent did the Papacy reform itself during the Counter Reformation?'
4. 'What was the contribution of the Papacy in countering the Reformation in the sixteenth century?'

Two of the questions require an overview of the whole topic. Which are they? Which question could mislead you into concentrating on the 'reform of the Papacy' if you are not careful?

Prepare a plan for answering question 1. Use your analysis of what was reformed to provide the framework. Your brief introduction should explain why reform was necessary, and your conclusion should include comments on what remained to be done after 1549.

Source-based questions on 'The Reform of the Papacy'

1 Adrian VI and reform, 1522–3
Read the extract from Adrian VI's statement, page 22, and the epitaph on his grave, page 24. Answer the following questions:

a) Why was Adrian's statement likely to have caused alarm within the Curia?
b) What two reasons did Adrian give for wishing to reform the Papacy?

c)   How far does Adrian's epitaph explain why he achieved so little reform?
d)   Was the writer of the epitaph sympathetic or unsympathetic to Adrian? Explain your answer.

2 *Consilium de emendenda ecclesia*, 1537

Read the two extracts from the *Consilium de emendenda ecclesia* given on pages 26 and 27. Answer the following questions:

a)   What is the meaning of the terms 'simony', 'right of collation', 'regresses', 'expectatives', and 'reservations', as used in the second extract?
b)   What criticism is made of exemptions in the first extract?
c)   How accurate is it to describe the two extracts as 'aggressively critical of abuses'?
d)   What does the author of the extracts hope will be achieved by the correction of the abuses he describes?
e)   How realistic was the programme of reforms outlined in the *Consilium de emendenda ecclesia*? (Use your wider knowledge of the topic in answering this question.)

3 Paul III (1534–49) and Sixtus V (1585–90)

Study the portraits of Paul III on the front cover, and of Sixtus V on page 34. Answer the following questions:

a)   What impression of Paul III is the artist attempting to create? Explain your answer.
b)   How far does the portrait substantiate the opinion of Paul III that you have already formed?
c)   Compare the two portraits. What are the similarities? What does this suggest about the conventions used in papal portraiture? What are the differences? Explain them.
d)   Sixtus V's portrait is surrounded by illustrations of his achievements. What was the general nature of these achievements, as presented by the illustrator? How accurate an assessment was this likely to be? Explain your answer.

CHAPTER 4

The Council of Trent

1 Background

When Martin Luther was attempting to defend his actions and his beliefs before the Emperor, Charles V, in 1520, he claimed that it was not the Pope who should finally pass judgement on him. He wished to appeal to a general council of the Church. He argued that such a council, and not the Pope, was the final arbiter of all disputes within the Church. This contention was politically astute, for by arguing in this way he focused on the issue that had been a major cause of disagreement between the rulers of Germany, lay and clerical, and the Papacy for generations. What is more, he was clearly taking the Emperor's side in the dispute, thus making it less likely that Charles V would act decisively against him.

The ploy was successful. Although the Emperor declared that Luther was wrong to have acted as he had, the steps taken to discipline him were less Draconian than the Pope desired, and they were ineffective. Charles V's policy was, and remained for more than 20 years, that a general council should be convened to resolve this and other outstanding issues. He maintained that the actions he took in the meantime were merely interim measures aimed at upholding the status quo.

Why was there so much controversy over the issue of the general council, and why did it take so long for the matter to be resolved? Clearly, there was much more at stake than the desirability of convening a meeting of leading churchmen from all parts of the Catholic world to discuss matters of mutual concern. It was accepted by all sides in the argument that the issue was really about where supreme authority in the Church lay. For centuries Popes had claimed that this authority was theirs, handed down from Jesus to the apostle Peter who was claimed to be the first Pope, and thence to each holder of the office in succession. A large number of lay and clerical leaders, especially in Italy, had long accepted this claim, but further afield from Rome it had been traditional to dispute it. In France and Germany in particular, the aspirations of the Papacy to supreme authority in the Church had been resisted. The Sorbonne (the University of Paris) had normally led the way in challenging papal claims. The Kings of France and the Emperors, generally supported by the rulers of Spain and the British Isles, had tended to champion the claims of the conciliarists. These were people who argued that the highest authority in the Church was a general council of the Church, although such a council had no recognised composition and no tradition of regular meetings.

The dispute was not just one about theory – it had highly significant practical implications. If the Papacy's claims were upheld, there would be no justification for lay rulers who resisted papal demands for the power to make the final decision in disputes over Church law, dogma, appointments, Church organisation, or any other issue relating to the religious life of Catholic states. However, if the papal claims could be resisted, rulers would be able to argue that they had as much right as the Pope to exercise political and financial control over the Church within their own territories. In particular it would give the lie to the long-held (but rarely stated) papal contention that lay rulers should be under the authority of the Church in all matters. This papal claim had been pressed with considerable success on several occasions during the Middle Ages, and it remained a potential weapon in the Papacy's diplomatic armoury well into the sixteenth century.

* In the early fifteenth century the conciliarists had achieved great success, as a result of the factionism into which the Papacy had dissolved in the late fourteenth century. On occasions each faction had elected its own Pope who had operated in competition with one or two others. In this situation both the credibility and the political power of the Papacy had been at a very low ebb, giving those who wished to rescue the Church from the grip of what seemed to be a political clique in Rome an opportunity to rally the forces opposed to papal supremacy. The outcome had been a series of general councils which had taken unto themselves ultimate responsibility within the Church. Each council had only met spasmodically and over a number of years. Yet, given the difficulties of travel in medieval Europe, it had been a remarkable achievement for the meetings to take place at all. The most famous of these general councils met in Constance (in modern day West Germany, close to the Swiss frontier) between 1414 and 1418. The city was conveniently situated between Italy, France and Germany. This had been important in ensuring that something approaching representative attendance had been achieved. The Council of Constance's most significant acts had been its declaration that a general council was the supreme authority in the Church; its deposition of the existing competing Popes on the grounds of invalid election, followed by the selection of a single Pope to replace them; and it decision that general councils should be summoned frequently in the future.

The remarkable successes of the conciliarists at the time of Constance had not been consolidated. The Papacy was, quite naturally, hostile to the aspirations of the movement, and it was in a first class position to ensure that the momentum was lost. In particular, it could do this by delaying the summoning of further councils. As there was general agreement that the Pope was the supreme ruler of the Church when a council was not in session, the Papacy had a strong vested interest in the failure of the conciliar movement. The conciliarists had all the disadvantages. They were effectively leaderless, being made up of churchmen and rulers from a wide variety of states, many of which were antagonistic to one another. Of special significance was the long struggle between France and the Holy Roman Empire for the political control of northern Italy. From 1494 onwards it was very unlikely that the Papacy would be faced by a united front of opposition from the major Catholic states as they were too busy fighting each other. Without this united opposition, it was almost certain that the Papacy would be able to continue with its policy of 'divide and rule' in Church matters.

By the early sixteenth century Popes had become terrified even at the possibility of their being a general council. Each Pope realised that there was sufficient evidence of corruption in his election and in his exercise of power for a general council to be justified in deposing him and selecting a replacement. On the basis of experience with past general councils, it was almost certain that irresistible demands would be made at any future council for the reform of the Papacy. There seemed everything to be lost and nothing to be gained from allowing a general council to meet. All that was required was for the Pope to promise to summon a council whenever demands for one became particularly insistent, and then to rely upon the political situation to provide valid excuses for a complete lack of action. After all, nothing short of a miracle would induce the Emperor and the King of France to agree on the time, the place, or the method of working of any council that was proposed. It was always possible to attach the blame for inactivity to somebody else.

The rivalry between the Habsburgs and the Valois was of great value to Popes who wished to avoid the calling of a general council. Although the Kings of France frequently threatened to agree to the calling of a council as a lever in diplomatic dealings with the Papacy, it was readily seen to be a bluff. For once Charles V was known to be a strong supporter of a meeting of a general council, pinning his hopes of solving the Lutheran problem on this happening, it was almost certain that France would do all in its power to prevent it. The existence of malcontented Protestant states within the Empire, with their potential for diverting and weakening the Emperor was too important an asset for the Kings of France to lose. Thus, while the Papacy was unwilling to summon a general council, and while France was willing to conspire to support this reluctance, there was virtually no possibility that a properly constituted general council would meet.

2 Paul III

Under Paul III the situation changed (see also pages 25–31). In 1536 he became convinced that unless vigorous action was taken to reform the Church both 'in its head and in its members' there was a real danger that it would cease to exist as an international institution. Of course, it is difficult to appreciate the papal fears of the mid-1530s from a modern day standpoint. Whereas we know that the Catholic Church not only survived but continued to have considerable international significance for centuries, Paul III had good reason to suspect that the end was near. It was 'common knowledge' (although inaccurate) at the time that the whole of Germany was likely to be lost to the Lutherans, and that the outward spread of Protestantism was virtually irresistible under current conditions. France and England seemed to be following in Germany's footsteps. However, the evidence that appears to have been critical in convincing Paul of the need for determined action was contained in the reports that Protestantism was winning numerous converts week by week in many Italian towns and cities. It seemed a realistic possibility that the Church would lose its 'homeland'.

Some of Paul's advisers, who shared his fears for the future, were not persuaded that the summoning of a general council was the best way forward. They thought that it would be sufficient for the Papacy to put its own house in order, by eliminating the abuses that emanated from Rome, and then to put pressure on the rulers of Europe to ensure that reforms took place in the localities. This strategy, they argued, would ensure that the initiative remained in papal hands and that there would be no challenge to papal supremacy. The approach was superficially very attractive, but in Paul's view it was unlikely to be effective. He knew that too many Catholics sympathised with the complaints of the Protestants for them not to be given a hearing. It was only when the Protestants had shown themselves unprepared to return to 'the fold' under reasonable terms, and when the differences between the two groups had been clearly defined that the Church would be able to mount an effective resistance to the spread of heresy. Paul recognised that a general council was the only appropriate forum in which this could be done, as well as being necessary to exert moral pressure on rulers who would be unwilling to implement reforms in their territories at the Pope's behest. He, therefore, saw the summoning of a council as the lesser of two evils – although he relished the prospect of neither. It is hardly surprising that at times his resolve weakened and that he was prepared to delude himself that, after all, inactivity might continue to be the best policy. But these lapses were usually of short duration and were no more than temporary aberrations in an otherwise consistent effort to secure the meeting of a general council.

* It took Paul almost a decade (1536–45) to translate intention into reality. In the fast-moving modern world, with immediate electronic communications, it is natural to interpret such a delay as a clear indication of a lack of serious intent. But this was not the case. Nearly all the difficulties that had allowed Popes to delay for several generations remained once the decision was made to summon a general council at last. In particular there was the need to win the agreement of the major temporal rulers. Unless this was done no council could take place. Although it was generally accepted (except by Charles V) that only the Pope was empowered to summon such a council, it was equally certain that it was in the power of local rulers to prevent both the summons being circulated in their territories and the movement of churchmen out of the country to attend the council. In practice, two rulers could exercise what was in effect a veto.

Charles V, through his direct rule of Spain, the Netherlands and southern Italy and his great influence in Germany, controlled such a large portion of the Catholic lands that it was inconceivable that a general council could be held without his active support. Fortunately for Paul, this support was generally forthcoming. But it was by no means a simple matter nor one to be taken for granted. Although Charles was genuinely committed to the Catholic Church and was determined to play his part in ensuring its survival, he was also a shrewd politician, energetic in his efforts to further the personal and dynastic ambitions that he had acquired in his youth. He was normally able to arrange matters so that it was possible to pursue both policies simultaneously, but at times there were tensions between the two. So Paul could not count on Charles's support for his plans. That support had to be won. Once Charles realised that the Pope was now keenly in favour of the meeting of a general council, rather than being opposed to it, he attempted to extract a political price for his support. He thought it reasonable that the Papacy should abandon its neutrality in the struggle between the Habsburgs and the Valois, especially as the French had allied with the common enemy, the Turks. This Paul was not prepared to do, knowing that if he were to take an anti-French stance, he would not only risk the Papacy falling under total Habsburg domination, but he would also destroy any realistic possibility of a general council actually meeting. Charles, however, remained unwilling to give up the possibility of gaining a political advantage from the situation. He continued to place annoying difficulties in Paul's way as long as he retained the hope that the Pope's resolution might weaken and that he might be prepared to make concessions in return for imperial support over the council.

The second effective veto rested with the King of France. He was the only ruler besides Charles V who controlled sufficient Catholic territory to make any general ecclesiastical decisions beyond his own lands. As far as Paul was concerned it was crucial that there should be French representation at the council. But if Charles V presented Paul with difficulties, then Francis I faced him with impossibilities. Although Francis was a committed Catholic, he was in no doubt that his first duty was to protect national and dynastic interests, which were synonymous in his mind. He was convinced that his enemy, Charles V, would be weakened as long as the Protestants remained a strong and potentially disruptive force in Germany. As it was generally believed that one of the main purposes of the proposed general council was to resolve the Protestant issue, it was only natural that Francis I should see little but loss for himself were the council actually to meet. His opposition was, therefore, likely to be automatic unless Paul could buy his support with some political concession. But Paul was in a poor position to do this. He had little that was of interest to Francis, besides siding with him in the struggle with the Habsburgs. This was too high a price to pay. So Paul had no choice but to await the time when changed circumstances would make it advantageous for Francis to lend his support to the meeting of the proposed general council.

* However, there were matters of significant detail that Paul could attempt to settle while he waited for the general political situation to swing in his favour. The most contentious issue was that of the venue for the meeting. This was largely a matter of national pride, with the French and the Germans each wishing to gain the prestige that would follow from the council being held in their territory. But there was a more serious dimension to the issue. It was assumed that the ruler in whose territory the council met would be able to exert significant influence over its deliberations. Paul would have liked a venue within the Papal States. This was totally unacceptable to Charles V who had often stated publicly that the next general council would be held 'on German soil'. This commitment, which Charles V was loath to break, presented Paul with some difficulties. A venue in Germany 'proper', to the north of the Alps, was likely to be unacceptable to the French, who would expect the council to be held in 'neutral' territory at worst, outside the control of any of the three major protagonists – the Pope, the Emperor, and the King of France. In addition, a venue some distance from the Papal States would present significant security risks and communication problems to the Pope or his representatives. What was needed was a city that was technically within the Empire, and thus 'on German soil', but which was sufficiently independent to be acceptable as neutral. As far as Paul was concerned, it also had to be securely Catholic, in no sense under threat from the Protestants.

Fortunately for Paul, such a city existed. Trent was an independent bishopric, whose Prince-Bishop owed no more than nominal allegiance to anybody. Although it is well within modern day Italy, in the sixteenth century it was recognised as being within the boundary of the Empire, and thus part of 'Germany'. Equally, it was close to the northern boundary of the Papal States and was therefore acceptable to the Pope. It was further from France than the French desired but there was no nearer alternative south of the Alps. The Swiss cities that had been acceptable compromise venues in the fifteenth century were under too much threat from the Protestants to be serious contenders. So, from the time of Paul's decision to summon a general council it appeared likely that Trent would be the site. Other possibilities were canvassed in the hope of securing more general agreement, especially from the French, but all other contenders had more and greater disadvantages. Trent was widely recognised as being the least bad of the possibilities, despite the facts that it was often bitterly cold in winter and was not generously endowed with suitable accommodation for the large number of Church leaders, many with extensive retinues, who were expected to attend the council. It would clearly be necessary to utilise accommodation at some distance from this city of 7,000–8,000 people, with only 1,500 houses.

    ★ Another vexed issue was the way in which decisions were to be reached by the council. In the general councils of the fifteenth century a system of 'voting by nations' had been adopted. In this system each 'nation' had had one vote on each issue, irrespective of the number of delegates in attendance. A nation's vote was cast on the side supported by the majority of its representatives. 'Nations' were not synonymous with independent political states. They were long-established and notional groupings based on the settlement pattern of the tribes that had invaded western Europe in the centuries following the break-up of the Roman Empire. The most populous of these nations was Germany. 'Voting by nations' had been designed to ensure that the council was not dominated by the geographical section of the Church that happened to be closest to the venue of the council and was thus able to be well represented.

    From the outset of discussions about the possibility of convening a general council, Paul III was determined that voting by nations should be discontinued. In the absence of clear evidence on the subject, it is only possible to guess at his motives. However, based on what is known about his other views, it is reasonable to speculate that he was eager to reduce the possibility of effective blocking by antagonistic sections of the Church that had only token representation at the meetings, but which, because of the voting system, were able to oppose measures that the Papacy advocated. He was confident that the majority of those who made the effort to attend the council would be committed to the changes that he wished to see taking place in the Church. No coherent opposition to his views on voting systems was mounted, and a general acceptance of individual voting was relatively easily established.

    However, there were complications. Some rulers assumed that they would be able to operate a 'block vote' system, with perhaps only one of their bishops attending the council, but carrying with him the proxy votes of his absent colleagues. As Charles V was one of these rulers, Paul III was immediately alerted to the danger posed by such an arrangement. He realised that the use of proxy votes would present the major territorial rulers with enormous power, in that they would be able to use their ability to sway the decisions of the council as a lever in the complex game of international politics that was certain to provide the backdrop to any council that actually met. Paul was, therefore, quick to establish the principles that voting would be by individual and that it would depend on attendance. He also insisted that the only people entitled to vote would be archbishops, bishops, and the heads of recognised religious orders. Thus, although monarchs and other lay rulers would be welcome to attend the council in person, or to be represented by ambassadors and learned theologians, they would have no more than an advisory capacity. He was determined that decisions would be made by those who held responsible positions within the Church, although he fully recognised that many such people were merely the creatures of the lay rulers who had appointed them. But many were not, and this gave Paul hope that a council might retain some political independence.

* Paul was in no doubt about the importance of retaining the initiative on all matters relating to the council. He knew that a council that was not firmly under the Pope's control was likely to present a real threat to papal interests. Once he had made the decision that the convening of a general council was essential to avoid the disintegration of the Church, he worked hard to make certain that detailed arrangements were made according to his wishes. He successfully resisted the claim by the Protestants that the Emperor had as much right to summon a council as did the Pope by persuading Charles V that the summons must come from the Pope. He obtained the agreement of the major rulers to his contention that the sessions of the council should be chaired by Papal Legates (the Pope's personally chosen representatives) who would have the power to decide on the order of business and to rule on all procedural matters. He was even successful in gaining acceptance that the council would have the status of an advisory body, making recommendations to the Pope, which could be implemented or ignored as seemed best to the pontiff of the time. These decisions, made when there was no certainty that the council would ever even meet, were to have profound effects on subsequent events. Although they placed the Pope in firm control of events, in that he retained at least a veto in all situations, they made it possible for progress to be made once the council met. Because Paul III and most of his immediate successors were persuaded both of the need for change and of the desirability of proceeding with the maximum possible general support, the council was destined to become the focal point of the structural and doctrinal reformation of the Church, rather than being the elaborate public relations exercise that many people feared it would be.

3 The Pattern of the Council

Although Paul III worked assiduously to prepare the ground for the meeting of a general council, it was actually beyond his power to secure the agreement of both Charles V and Francis I as to its summoning. He had to accept that he could do no more than make things ready and then await the time when circumstances favoured his plans. This was likely to be when Charles and Francis were at peace with one another. As early as 1536 Paul thought that the time was right, and summoned the council to meet. However, it was soon apparent that he had been over-optimistic and that more careful preparation of the ground with

Charles and Francis was necessary. He therefore engineered a meeting with both monarchs at Nice in 1538 when the prospects of agreement seemed good. But his hopes were dashed. Both rulers retained expectations of victory over the other, and neither was prepared to make the compromises necessary to agree the time, the place, and the procedures for the meeting of the proposed council. In fact, Paul was only to see his plans come to fruition once Charles V had inflicted major military defeats on Francis I. Charles was then able to dictate to Francis the terms on which they would jointly support Paul in summoning a general council. This happened in 1544 when, in the Peace of Crepy, Francis I was forced to agree to a council being held.

At last there was the realistic prospect of the council actually meeting. However, after all the false hopes of the previous eight years it is hardly surprising that many churchmen were very sceptical about the likelihood of anything happening now. Despite Paul's urgings for attendance, the vast majority of those eligible to be present decided to play a waiting game, doing nothing until it was clear that there was to be action. The prospects were further damaged by Francis I's decision not to allow any of his bishops to attend the council to which he had only agreed under pressure. Thus when the Council of Trent was formally opened in December 1545 there were only 31 bishops in attendance. This was less than five per cent of those who were entitled to be present.

Such a beginning hardly augured well. Nor did the initial lengthy arguments about the order of business. These disagreements highlighted the fact that Charles V and Paul III had vastly different expectations of the Council. Charles viewed the Council in the context of his struggles with the Protestants. Even though the failure at Regensburg in 1541 (see page 28) had seriously undermined his confidence in the practicality of a negotiated settlement with the Lutherans, and had led him to suspect that the final answer might have to be military action, he still retained some hope that the deliberations of a general council might provide the solution. His expectation was that the Council would first take action to remove the abuses, mostly emanating from the Curia in Rome, about which both Protestants and Catholics in Germany had complained for so long. Charles was convinced that the removal of these abuses would stem the tide of defection from the Church within the Empire. He anticipated that the Council would then agree definitions of dogma (the beliefs of the Church) that were sufficiently inexact and generalised for both Catholics and Lutherans to be able to accept them.

Paul's perception was very different. He wished the Council to draw hard and fast lines between the beliefs that were acceptable within the Church and those that were to be regarded as heretical. His motives had nothing to do with seeking an accommodation with the Protestants. His desire was to erect effective defences against further Protestant attacks on the Church, and to challenge the Lutherans to return to the fold on his terms or to be damned. He considered that a careful definition of doctrine was the key to the problem. With this, Catholics would be able to identify both their friends and their enemies and would be able to take appropriate action. Abuses were clearly of secondary importance in this context.

A compromise was reached. It was decided that issues of discipline (in which most of the abuses lay) and definitions of dogma would be considered simultaneously. This apparently equal sacrifice by Pope and Emperor was actually a total rejection of Charles's strategy. He quickly came to understand that no answers to his problems would be found at Trent, and he increasingly lost interest in the events taking place there. Instead, he turned his attention to defeating the Protestants in battle. The non-attendance of both the French and the Protestants left the way clear for papal domination of the proceedings of the Council.

This domination was confirmed by the working practices of the Council. Issues were considered in an order decided by the Papal Legates. Each issue was discussed by the non-voting technical experts (the theologians) in the presence of the voting members for as long as the Legates thought appropriate. The Legates were able to ensure that the theologians who supported the Pope's point of view had the major, and especially the final say. The bishops then considered the matter and agreed on the exact wording of a decree which enshrined the Council's decision on the subject. Decrees had no validity until they had been approved by the Pope. Thus it was virtually impossible for the Council to reach any conclusion with which the Pope was not in complete agreement. It is little wonder that most Popes wished to continue the Council for as long as possible.

The Council of Trent met in three distinct periods over a span of 18 years, from December 1545 to December 1563. During this time meetings were actually held in 25 sessions of varying length, lasting in total about four years. The first period, technically from December 1545 to September 1549, (but in practice suspended from 1547), was during Paul III's pontificate. It was made up of eight sessions, during which major steps were taken towards an exact definition of the teachings of the Church. This was despite the fact that intense political manoeuvrings were going on in the background. At one stage the very existence of the Council was seriously threatened. Paul, assuming that Charles V's attention was totally dominated by the successful military campaign he was conducting against the Protestant states of the Empire, decided in May 1547 to move the Council to Bologna, which was within the Papal States. His excuse was that an outbreak of cholera in Trent made it unsafe for the Council to continue there. Charles interpreted this action as a blatant attempt by the Pope to secure domination of the Council's proceedings. He instructed his subjects to remain at Trent, which they did. This effectively brought the work of the Council to a halt. In the end Paul III, recognising that no further progress would be made in the near future, allowed the Council to adjourn with no agreed date for re-convening.

The Council's second period, May 1551 to April 1552, was made up of six sessions. Paul III had died in November 1549, and the meetings were held under the auspices of his successor, Julius III. Little of note was achieved. The problem was a lack of direction from the Papacy, which was content to adopt the negative role of ensuring that no compromises were made by the Council which might assist Charles V in his continuing search for an agreement with the Protestants. Charles had decisively defeated the Protestants in battle in 1547, but he realised that there could be no permanent settlement with them until they were allowed to rejoin the Church on acceptable terms. He now hoped that the Council would be able to agree those acceptable terms. But he was too late. The first period, and the early months of the second period of the Council had adopted definitions of faith that made any agreement with the Protestants impossible (see pages 53–7), and although Charles was able to ensure that Lutheran representatives attended the later sessions of the second period, he was unable to influence events sufficiently to avoid the anticipated breakdown of negotiations. It was now clear for all to see that there could no longer be any realistic expectation of reaching an accommodation between the Catholic and Protestant points of view.

There was a nine year gap between the second and third periods of the Council. In part this was caused by Carafa's pontificate as Paul IV (1555–9). Carafa was hostile to the very concept of a general council, maintaining that the Pope was well able to introduce the reforms that were necessary, both of discipline and dogma, on his own authority, without having to seek the agreement of others. His successor, Pius IV (1559–65), wished to complete the work begun by Paul III, and he was responsible for reconvening the Council for its final eleven sessions from January 1562 to December 1563. These sessions were the crowning success for the Council. Attendance was relatively good, (a maximum of 235 voting members compared with 72 and 59 in the first two periods respectively), especially as there was a significant French contingent. The work commenced in the first period was completed. In particular, detailed proposals were framed to ensure that the good intentions of the first period were now likely to be translated into action. It was in the third period that the significant steps towards the reform of church discipline were taken.

*Although the Council of Trent retained a single identity, it lacked coherence in many respects. This was unavoidable given that attendance at the Council was not consistent. No one was present throughout, the Papal Legates were different in each period, and the representation from the different geographical regions of the Church was very variable. Nevertheless, the statistics reveal a clear pattern. A total of

270 bishops attended the Council at one time or another. 187 of these were from Italy, 31 were from Spain, 26 were from France (almost all in the third period), and only 2 were from Germany. The overwhelming Italian attendance at the Council might be interpreted as yet more evidence of papal domination. However, it would be a mistake to assume that papal control was absolute. Whereas it is correct to claim that all the actions of the Council had to receive papal approval before they acquired effective status, this did not mean that the Popes initiated every move. Although there was very close contact between the Popes and their legates, with detailed daily reports and sets of instructions passing between Trent and Rome during the third period, the legates were by no means cyphers. Each had views of his own and they managed to establish in the minds of those attending Trent that the legates were to some extent 'neutral chairmen'. They clearly had papal interests and policies at heart, but they exercised some independence of judgement. This was, of course, essential to the establishment of the legates' credibility in the eyes of the bishops attending the Council. Nor were all of the Italian bishops open to influence from the Pope, although many were as they depended on papal pensions to eke out the meagre incomes they received from their dioceses. The bishops from most of southern Italy were as much under Habsburg influence as were those from Spain, while the sizeable contingent from Venetian territory were the inheritors of a strong anti-papal tradition. The fact that no Pope personally visited the Council is confirmation that the Papacy's control of events was at least at one remove.

4 The Teachings of the Church

The approach of the Council of Trent to matters of dogma are the best justification for the use of the term 'Counter Reformation'. Throughout the three periods of the Council the intention appears to have been to identify in detail the theological differences between Protestants in general, and Lutherans in particular, and the Catholic Church. These differences were then explored exhaustively and statements were made which clearly established the dividing lines between them. Those who accepted teachings that were on the Protestant side of these lines were declared to be heretics, damned to exist outside the Church's fold. Even the form taken by the decisions of the Council revealed its anti-Protestant intentions. On each theological topic there was a decree. Each decree was made up of two sections: a lengthy explanation of the Church's standpoint divided into chapters, and a series of pithy statements called canons, each of which detailed a Protestant belief that Catholics should reject. But it was not only what was done and the way in which it was approached that provided clear evidence of the 'counter reformation' intentions of the Council members. What was not done was equally revealing. No time was spent on defining dogma in those areas where there were no disputes between Protestants and Catholics. So it is apparent that the intention was not to decide in detail all that Catholics should believe, but merely to make certain that Protestant teachings were outlawed.

The establishment of hard and fast dividing lines between what was acceptable and what was anathema to the Church appealed only to hard-line Catholics. It was essentially a reactionary process. It was intended by its supporters to force those who were sympathetic to some aspects of Protestant teachings to declare themselves for one side or the other. In particular, it put pressure on those liberal Catholics who had enjoyed a political ascendancy in Rome for much of the 1520s and 1530s to abandon their moderate stance and to identify themselves with the traditional teachings of the Church. But the triumph of such antagonistic views was not a foregone conclusion at the Council. There were powerful groupings who wished the Council to assume a unifying rather than a divisive role. Those bishops who received their instructions from Charles V were horrified at the anti-Protestant intentions that were immediately revealed by the Papal Legates. Less concerned initially were those theologians who recognised that the biblical studies undertaken by Protestants and Catholics alike in the previous decades had revealed the need to adjust some of the Church's existing teachings. They assumed that their views would prevail. Within a short time, however, they came to understand that they were to stand as rejected as the Protestants. They argued long and hard but they were outmanoeuvred by the Legates at every turn. Traditionally-minded theologians, especially Jesuits, were used at key moments by the Legates to make telling contributions that swayed the members of the Council. On every issue traditional views triumphed over those newer teachings that had their roots in the researches of the humanists, who were largely discredited at Trent.

Much to the surprise of most observers, it was during the first 18 months of the Council, up to late spring 1547, that the most significant work on dogma was done. This meant that two expectations were not met. Papal opposition to the calling of a council had for long been based on the assumption that any general council would spend much of its time attempting to wrest control of the Church from the Pope. Although somewhat feeble efforts in this direction were made during the early sessions of the first period at Trent, the Legates had little difficulty in directing attention away from this most contentious area. Thanks to such skilful deflective action, the Council operated with a tacit acceptance of papal supremacy, without ever explicitly resolving the issue. Equally shrewdly, the programme of work was planned so as to give the appearance of honouring the agreement with Charles V, whereby issues of dogma and of discipline would be tackled simultaneously, but in effect the concentration was on the teachings of the Church, as the Pope wished.

a) The Sources of Christian Truth

Concentration was immediately directed at the key areas of disagreement with the Protestants. One of the most important of these was the teaching related to the sources of Christian truth. Martin Luther, in common with almost all Protestant theologians, was absolutely convinced that the Bible contained the only evidence of God's message to mankind. This view was encapsulated in his teaching of *scriptura sola* (scripture alone). Protestants used this teaching as a reason for rejecting many Catholic beliefs, arguing that if a belief could not be substantiated directly from the Bible it was not only unjustified but was probably also the work of the Devil. Catholics countered this argument by claiming that God's message had also been communicated in ways other than through the Bible. They contended, in particular, that there had been revelations to early Christians which had been passed down as traditions within the Church, and which were just as valid as the biblical message. In April 1546 the Council agreed a decree on the subject. Among other things, it stated that:

1 This truth and way of living are contained in written books and in unwritten traditions, which were received by the Apostles from the mouth of Christ himself, or were received by the same Apostles at the dictation of the Holy Spirit, and, as it were, passed
5 on from hand to hand until they came down to us. So, following the example of the orthodox fathers, this Council receives and venerates, with equal pious affection and reverence, all the books both of the New and the Old Testaments, since one God is author of both, together with the said traditions, as well as those
10 pertaining to faith as those pertaining to morals, as having been given either from the lips of Christ or by the dictation of the Holy Spirit and preserved by unbroken succession in the Catholic Church.

This was an essential first step in the defence of existing Catholic beliefs and practices in the face of Protestant attack.

    * However, a large part of Catholic opposition to Luther's stance was a result of the Church hierarchy's dislike of the way in which the Protestants elevated the individual believer at the expense of the officials of the Church, from priest to Pope. Luther did this by encouraging the individual Christian to form his own beliefs by a careful and prayerful study of the text of the Bible. His message was that the Holy Spirit would guide the pious seeker after truth, and that there was no need for the Church to tell people what to believe. This teaching undermined the entire system of authority and control within the Catholic Church. It needed to be discredited. The Council was quick to do this. It decreed that the interpretation of the scriptures was

not an appropriate activity for the individual church member:

1 No one, relying on his own judgement and twisting sacred
  Scripture to his own ends, should dare to interpret sacred
  Scripture in a way contrary to the sense which holy Mother
  Church (whose office it is to judge the true sense and interpreta-
5 tion of the sacred Scriptures) has held and now holds, or in a way
  which is contrary to the unanimous agreement of the Fathers of
  the Church.

However, although this approach was followed up to some extent, it
was not pursued as far as some of the more reactionary Catholics
wished. Official disapproval was obtained for the biblical research that
had been undertaken by leading humanists such as Erasmus. The
recent Catholic translations of the Bible from its original Hebrew and
Greek into Latin were ignored and the ancient translation by St Jerome,
known as the Vulgate, was confirmed as the official translation to be
used within the Church. This was despite the fact that nearly all men of
learning accepted that the Vulgate was full of errors. The conservatives
were in a quandary. Once they accepted that errors had been made in
the past they were in danger of being swept towards Protestant
positions by the force of recent scholarship. They considered that the
lesser of the evils was to turn their backs entirely on the findings of
biblical research. But they were not successful in their attempts to
secure the banning of translations other than the Vulgate, nor even in
their determination to outlaw all vernacular translations of the Bible.
The forces of liberal Catholicism were sufficiently strong within the
Council to resist the attempt to shut off obedient Catholics from all
contact with alternative versions of the Word of God, even though they
were unable to stem the tide of theological conservatism that was
ensuring that no compromises would be made with Protestant positions. Such was the conservative ethos of the Council that the liberal
Catholics considered it a victory that the reading of the Bible in people's
native languages was not banned: it was too much to hope that they
would win actual approval for the activity.

b) The Teaching on Salvation

The second main plank of Protestantism, upon which so much else
rested, was the teaching on salvation and how it was obtained. Catholics
and Protestants alike viewed life on earth as a relatively brief – and
generally miserable – interlude in the existence of the eternal soul that
was in each human being. Mortal life's prime purpose as far as
Catholics were concerned was to provide God with evidence of the
soul's fitness to enjoy eternal life in heaven. They claimed that it was
possible for the individual to make his soul acceptable to God by living

a good life and by building up enough 'merit' to outweigh the 'demerit' attracted by his sinfulness. Protestants entirely rejected this view. Luther's teaching of *sola fide* (by faith alone) maintained that man is so sinful that no action by him could justify himself in the eyes of a God who requires perfection, and that salvation can only come as the result of God's freely and undeservedly given forgiveness. He taught that no human actions can affect the granting of God's grace.

The implications of the Catholic teachings on salvation were considerable. A large amount of the Church's dogma depended on the efficacy of good works. It was their ability to bestow merit on the recipient that gave special significance to the seven sacraments of the Church (baptism, confirmation, matrimony, extreme unction, penance, ordination, and the Eucharist). A similar accumulation of merit was believed to be attached to the veneration of saints, as on pilgrimages; to the purchase of indulgences, whether for oneself or for a loved one; to devoting one's life to God as a member of a religious community; and to the carrying out of charitable deeds, especially for the sake of those who had taken a vow of poverty. If, as the Protestants claimed, the individual could not increase the likelihood of salvation by his own endeavours, then much of the point of religious activity was removed. It was therefore essential for the Council to confirm the Church's teaching on these matters, and to discredit the beliefs popularised by Luther.

The Council spent most of the second half of 1546 debating these issues in detail. The first task was to establish the exact nature of original sin. Underpinning Luther's thinking about salvation was his assumption that mankind was utterly sinful. He contended that each person inherited such a burden of sin at birth – handed down from generation to generation, following Adam's fall in the Garden of Eden as described in the Old Testament – that it was impossible for anybody to become virtuous by his own efforts. He must, therefore, depend upon God's cleansing grace, made freely available to mankind as a result of Jesus's death and resurrection. Luther argued that compared with the huge deficit of merit with which each person entered the world, the strivings of the good person throughout life were as nothing. It seemed self-evident to him that salvation must come as a result of something other than individual virtue. The Council was determined to refute this Protestant teaching. This was done by accepting the existence of original sin, but by indicating the way in which it could be completely overcome, thus allowing the young Christian to begin his responsible life with a clean sheet. One of the canons of the decree on original sin stated:

1 If anyone should deny that the guilt of original sin is remitted through the grace of our Lord Jesus Christ conferred in baptism, or asserts that thereby everything which can truly and properly be

called sin is not taken away, but only covered or not imputed, let
5 him be anathema.

The detailed work on the teachings concerning justification (the way in
which salvation was acquired) was the most time-consuming of any of
the Council's tasks. The resulting decree, with 16 chapters and 33
canons, was the longest of the statements from Trent. In the decree,
and especially in the canons, the major Protestant teachings were
specifically refuted:

1 *Canon 12* If anyone should say that justifying faith is nothing
  other than trust in the divine mercy which remits sins for Christ's
  sake, or that we are justified by such trust alone, let him be
  anathema.
5 *Canon 26* If anyone should say that for their good works,
  performed in godly wise, the just ought not to expect and hope for
  an eternal reward from God, through his mercy and the merits of
  Jesus Christ – if they persevere to the end in good living and
  keeping the divine commandments – let him be anathema.
10 *Canon 32* If anyone should say that the good works of a justified
  man are so exclusively the gifts of God that they are not also the
  good merits of the man himself; or that the justified man, by the
  good works that he does through the grace of God and the merits
  of Jesus Christ (whose living member he is), does not truly merit
15 an increase of grace and eternal life . . . let him be anathema.

The opportunity was also taken to re-affirm those Catholic beliefs that
had come under particularly hostile attack from Luther and his
followers, who taught that the Church was attempting to terrify its
members with unwarranted threats so as better to control them:

1 *Canon 29* If anyone should say that a man who has fallen into sin
  after baptism cannot rise again through the grace of God; or that
  he can indeed recover his lost righteousness, but only by faith and
  without the sacrament of penance, so contradicting what the holy
5 Roman and universal Church, taught by Christ our Lord and his
  Apostles, has always professed, observed and taught, let him be
  anathema.
  Canon 30 If anyone should say that, for every penitent sinner
  who receives the grace of justification the wiping out of the guilt
10 and debt of eternal punishment means that there remains no debt
  of temporal punishment to be paid either in this world or in the
  next world in purgatory, before he can enter the kingdom of
  heaven, let him be anathema.

c) The Sacraments

During its first period the Council also dealt directly with issues relating to the seven sacraments, as well as confirming them obliquely within its statements on justification and on the sources of Christian truth. It was on the question of the sacraments that the Church felt most exposed by Protestant attacks. Luther's contention that only two of the sacraments (baptism and the Eucharist) were valid, being the only ones directly founded on scripture, had won widespread and ready support from ordinary people. It was an argument that was particularly difficult to counter as the justifications for the other five sacraments tended to be complex and obscure. They were not easy to popularise.

There was insufficient time during the productive months of the first period of the Council, up to the spring of 1547, to do more than make simple but explicit statements confirming the validity of all seven sacraments. The detailed work of closely defining and justifying each of them was undertaken in the second and third periods. The most bitterly contested disagreement between the Protestants and the Catholics had been over the nature and significance of the Eucharist (called holy communion by the Protestants), and it was this topic that provided the only significant achievement of the second period. In October 1551 a decree clarifying the Church's teaching on the Eucharist was agreed. It displayed a determined anti-Protestantism, making no effort to seek common ground on this most contentious issue. It was no wonder that when the Protestant delegates arrived at the Council shortly after the decree had been promulgated, they felt that they had been tricked into attendance by false promises of probable agreement. Nor was it surprising that Charles V, who had worked extremely hard to ensure a Protestant presence at Trent after 1547, should feel massively slighted that the ground had so blatantly been cut from under his feet. His subsequent efforts to reach an agreement with the Protestants away from the Council were perfectly understandable given the intransigent attitudes that prevailed at Trent.

Within the main body of the decree on the Eucharist it was stated:

1 Since Christ our Redeemer said that which he offered under the appearance of bread was truly his body, it has therefore always been held in the Church of God, and this holy Council now declares anew, that through consecration of the bread and wine
5 there comes about a conversion of the whole substance of the bread into the substance of the body of Christ our Lord and the whole substance of the wine into the substance of his blood. And this conversion is by the Holy Catholic Church conveniently and properly called transubstantiation.

This was an explicit rejection of all shades of Protestant teaching on the subject. Equally explicit was the rejection of Protestant claims that the way in which Catholics conducted mass (the service in which the Eucharist took place) was at best idolatrous:

1 *Canon 6*   If anyone should say that, in the holy sacrament of the Eucharist, Christ, the only-begotten Son of God, ought not to be adored with the worship of divine honour, outwardly manifested; and likewise that he ought not to be honoured with special
5 solemnity on festive occasions, nor borne about in processions, in accordance with the praiseworthy and universal rites and custom of the holy Church; or that he ought not to be publicly set before the people to be adored; or that those who thus adore him are idolaters, let him be anathema.

By the end of the third period of the Council, similarly clear and uncompromising statements had been made about all the sacraments and the practices that were associated with them. The traditional teachings of the Church had been confirmed in the face of Protestant attack, with no compromises being struck. Even the concessions that Charles V was prepared to make in order to reach an accommodation with the Lutherans were specifically outlawed. The majority of German-speaking Catholics sympathised with the Protestants in seeing no justification for either insisting on the celibacy of the priesthood or denying lay people the right to drink the wine during the Eucharist. Yet these practices were confirmed as obligatory, even in the face of considerable political pressure from the Church's leading lay supporters. It was to be seen that the Church was yielding no ground at all in response to the arguments of its religious opponents. Stubbornness was being made into a virtue.

5 Discipline

Of course, it was not only because of their wish to counter the spread of Protestantism that the Pope and the majority of the bishops attending the Council of Trent were eager to tackle questions of dogma before matters of discipline. Although issues about the Church's teachings generated very strong emotions – there were even cases of bishops who held opposite opinions physically attacking each other during meetings of the Council – and were regarded by some as being matters of eternal life and death, questions of dogma were, in fact, relatively 'safe' matters to debate. Neither the Pope nor those attending the Council felt that their livelihoods or their political powers were threatened by decisions made about the teachings of the Church. On the other hand, they were fearful that their vested interests would be under direct attack once matters of discipline came under consideration. After all, the complaints that had been so persistently voiced for more than a generation –

especially, but by no means exclusively, in Germany – were almost all directed at the Papacy and the higher clergy (bishops, archbishops, priors and abbots) in the localities. It was widely appreciated by all the delegates that they were likely to be materially and politically disadvantaged by any changes in Church discipline that the Council agreed.

Some reforming churchmen believed that such a price was well worth paying if the result was to be a spiritually revitalised Church. But at the outset such people were no more than a significant minority. The majority were very reluctant to contemplate changes that would work to their personal disadvantage. Altruism was not a prominent feature among those who influenced the decisions of the Council. In particular, all the Popes who were in office during the period of the Council of Trent were determined that it should not be allowed to interfere with the running of the Curia. Although there were differences of opinion among the Popes on the ways and means of reforming the Curia (see page 31) there was consistent and effective opposition to the idea of the Council playing any part in the process. The Papal Legates were instructed to ensure that decisions on matters of discipline were limited to topics that related to the workings of the Church in the localities. Powers exercised from Rome were only to be discussed where they were inextricably linked with the functioning of the Church in the provinces. Whereas the Council was to be allowed to play a part in the reform of the 'members', only the Pope was to be allowed to reform the 'head'.

However, there was a powerful current of opinion which favoured a reform of discipline. This did not result solely, or even primarily, from a desire to satisfy the Emperor and his Catholic supporters in Germany. It was a central feature of a coherent strategy for the revival of the Church that had been gaining support among leading churchmen, both in Rome and in some localities, especially in Italy and Spain, during the 1520s and 1530s. The most important element of the strategy was to strengthen the spiritual and political position of the bishops. It was believed that strong and effective leadership at diocesan level was the key to bringing about changes at all levels of Church life. Bishops were seen as being the facilitators of local reform. This view permeated the deliberations of all three periods of the Council. It was expressed in the Legate's speech at the opening of the first session, and it was the single most time-consuming issue during the third period of the Council. Progress was often painfully slow, because of the obstructive opposition of those who could only see themselves as being losers if the status quo was upset, but the cumulative achievement was amazingly great.

The biggest change, from which much else flowed, was one of attitude. Most holders of high office in the Church, except in Spain, had grown up thinking of bishoprics as prizes to be won. They were important because of the income or the political power that accompanied them. If there was any conception of associated responsibilities it was the recognition that somebody had to be employed, normally at a relatively lowly salary, to carry out some official duties on the bishop's behalf. There was little reason for a bishop ever to visit, let alone be resident in, his diocese. Some bishops did not even remember the names or know the locations of the bishoprics they held. During the period of the Council of Trent it became generally agreed among leading churchmen that this situation was unacceptable. The prevailing assumption became that the responsibilities of being a bishop were at least as important as its rewards. Thus the views of the reformers became the norm, and the opinions of those who resisted change were relegated to the realms of self-seeking reaction. This, however, is not to suggest that the path to reform was smooth or straightforward, for it was not. But it became more difficult for the supporters of the status quo to justify their position on the grounds that it had always been so.

The acceptance that the responsibilities of bishops were of central importance led naturally to the consideration of other issues. The responsibilities of the bishop needed to be clearly defined; the conditions under which the responsibilities could effectively be discharged needed to be identified and put into effect; and the attributes of the potentially successful bishop needed to be described and steps taken to ensure that only suitable people were appointed to such posts. Although the logic of such a process was compelling, and eventually proved irresistible, there was much agonising and time-wasting along the way. It was only during the Council's third period that the issues were dealt with in a coherent manner.

The Council of Trent defined the bishop as what in modern parlance would be termed a manager. His role was to ensure that religious life within his diocese was carried out in an acceptable manner. He was expected to supervise the work of the parish priests directly and to discipline those whose performance was unsatisfactory. He was to lead by example, especially by visiting every parish at least once every two years. He was to help overcome the shortage of priests who could preach effectively by taking on a large element of this work himself. Being a bishop was now assumed to be a full-time job.

It was readily recognised that much would have to change before bishops could be expected to act in this way. As a first step, they would have to live in their dioceses. Efforts were made in the productive months of the first period to ensure that bishops were not absentees in future. But the strength of the opposition meant that only a compromise ruling was made. In 1547 it was decreed that bishops should only be absent from their dioceses with good reason, and that if they were absent for more than six months without good reason they should sacrifice one quarter of their annual income. Thus a totally absentee bishop could still receive three-quarters of his stipend. The fact that, immediately following the decree, the Pope was unsuccessful in his attempts to send the many bishops resident in Rome to live in their dioceses, illustrates how little of a deterrent the decree was. But at least the principle of the desirability of the residence of bishops within their dioceses had been clearly established, and it was reinforced later when it was decreed that the income from a bishopric should only be paid to the person who carried out the duties of bishop. The intention was to outlaw the practice of the wealthy and well-connected being bishops in name, but paying for substitutes to act for them.

There had always been numbers of dedicated bishops who had attempted to carry out their duties effectively. They had often been frustrated in their efforts by the existence of widespread exemptions. Some of these exemptions were general, as with the various orders of friars where the whole group had been exempted from diocesan control by the Pope, who wished them to be directly accountable to their superiors within their own orders. Initially, most general exemptions had been allowed in the hope that this would lead to improved supervision and more consistent discipline, given that many bishops were unreliable and were only likely to interfere for reasons of self-interest. There were also large numbers of particular exemptions, whereby individuals had secured papal agreement to their removal from diocesan control – often in return for a large fee. Many of these individuals were non-practising clergy who merely wished to draw a clerical income in peace without aggravation from any over-zealous bishop. It was impossible for bishops to maintain effective discipline within their dioceses while such exemptions continued. One of the more significant disciplinary decrees of the Council instructed that exemptions should not apply to any clerical post that involved responsibility for the care of souls. Thus bishops were made directly responsible for all clergy who acted in the capacity of a parish priest within their dioceses. This decree made it theoretically possible for bishops to carry out the most important of their responsibilities. Almost equally as important as the ending of many exemptions was the decision to empower bishops to veto the appointment of any priest to a post involving the care of souls. This enactment allowed active bishops to ensure that future appointments within their diocese were of people who were capable of carrying out their duties effectively.

Just as it was necessary to increase the likelihood of effective parish priests being appointed, so it was vital that something be done about the competence of those who were appointed to bishoprics. The worst of the abuses were well-publicised and were little supported, in theory at least. There could be little justification for the political appointment of bishops who had no knowledge of or interest in religion, and who were often not even priests. It was worse when the person appointed was a child, and as such was clearly unable to undertake any of his official duties. The argument that all those appointed to bishoprics should be capable of carrying out their duties, both by age and training, was relatively easily accepted. However, the feeling that the rule applied to everybody but oneself was encouraged when the Pope appointed an eleven year old as a cardinal soon after accepting the Council's decree on the attributes of bishops! Nevertheless, the principle had been established that only appropriate people should be appointed as bishops.

It was during the third period of the Council that the major work on bishops was done. The Legates were able to ensure active support for their policies partly because of the presence of a significant number of Spanish bishops who were keenly interested in the reform of discipline. However, the Spanish support was a mixed blessing for the Papacy. The lengthy debates on the duties of bishops were the most dangerous times for papal interests during the whole Council. The Spanish not only shared the papal perception that the revival of the Church depended on the quality of the bishops serving it in the future, but they also maintained that all bishops were directly ordained by God and that their rights and obligations came from Him. As a result, they argued that the Pope, as Bishop of Rome, was merely *primus inter pares* (the first among equals) and, therefore, had no right to exercise power over the whole Church. The Legates had a difficult tight-rope to walk in ensuring the Spanish bishops' continuing support for the reform programme, while resisting their attacks on the papal position.

The success achieved in this, as well as the success achieved during the third period of the Council as a whole, was largely due to the political skills of the chief Papal Legate, Cardinal Morone. Morone possessed a rare combination of attributes. He had a clear, coherent, and unshakable vision of what the Council should achieve. Because he treated everyone with consideration and respect, he was personally acceptable in all circles, even among those who radically disagreed with what he was trying to achieve. He was, therefore, able to negotiate with all factions, which he did with shrewdness and a complete lack of scruples. He unashamedly traded favours, giving his support on a relatively insignificant issue in return for support on what was to him a vital matter. He was even prepared to leave the Council in order to pay a personal visit to the Emperor, and so partake in direct negotiations on particularly sensitive issues. As a result of the Cardinal's journey, the Emperor was prepared to abandon his support of policies which were aimed at molifying the Protestants in return for a papal promise of support for the election of his son as King of the Romans (the title that ensured that the holder would be the next Emperor).

★ Although the attention of the Council on disciplinary matters was clearly focused on the role of the bishop, the importance of the parish priest was not overlooked. In fact, the provision of an adequate supply of properly trained and positively motivated priests was recognised as being of the greatest significance. This, at least, had been learned from the Protestants. It was again decided to rely upon the bishops as facilitators. It was decreed that every bishop should arrange for a seminary (a training institution for priests) to be established within his diocese, if one did not already exist, as it had been correctly estimated that a sufficient supply of new priests could not be provided by the existing university system. However, the decision was not entirely forward-looking. There was a lengthy struggle over the nature of the academic training to be given to the prospective priests. The more progressive reformers wanted students to receive a thorough grounding in the Bible and scriptural criticism, at the expense of the traditional scholastic approach which was based on the application of logic to largely unquestioned basic Catholic teachings. The traditionalists won. As a result, the revitalised Catholic Church turned its back on academic progress, and for centuries was associated with an unthinking conservatism that many observers have seen as being somewhat at odds with the fundamentally radical Christian message.

Just as the Council attempted to give clear guidance on the attributes and activities of bishops, so it tried to provide similar definitions for parish priests. Bishops were instructed on the expectations they should have of those serving under them, in terms of their skills, their knowledge and the quality of the lives they lived. An emphasis was placed on their ability to preach successfully, and to live in a way that would be a good example to their flocks. However, as in the case of bishops, the issues of absenteeism and pluralism were tackled in a half-hearted manner that left loopholes through which the nominal priest could escape. But the decrees on these matters should not be dismissed as being unimportant merely because they allowed the continuation of some abuses. They were of special importance because they helped to establish an atmosphere in which good service from a priest was expected and in which any deviation from this was considered to be a shortcoming.

6 Significance

It is hardly surprising that many historians have judged the Council of Trent to be of the greatest significance. It was, after all, the one 'event' of the Counter Reformation that was discrete, coherent, and extremely well documented. In fact, it would be amazing if researchers had not regarded the Council as the topic's most important 'happening'. As always in such situations, however, the student must consider carefully whether the event had real historical significance or whether the interest of historians is merely a reflection of the ready availability of evidence.

The criteria normally used by historians in discussing the significance of an event concentrate on its effects. For convenience, these are often divided into short-term and long-term effects. There has been general agreement that, according to such criteria, the Council was highly significant. However, as might be expected, there has been some disagreement over the relative importance of the various effects.

It was commonplace several generations ago for historians to assert that one of the most important short-term effects of the Council was to make it impossible for there to be any agreement with the Protestants, leading to a re-unification of the Church. The argument was that the anti-Protestant definitions of dogma agreed by the Council destroyed the prospects for a religious peace, of the type that Charles V had championed. In more recent times this view has been discredited. It is now widely accepted that long before the Council met, any realistic hope of a *rapprochement* between the Protestants and the Catholics had disappeared. Charles V's efforts had proved that the minimum terms demanded by the Lutherans – including a rejection of papal supremacy – were totally unacceptable to the large majority of Catholics. It is clear that the Council merely formalised an already existing situation.

However, historians are agreed that the work of the Council in drawing hard and fast lines between Catholic and Protestant teachings was highly significant in the short-term for other reasons. Until the publication of the Tridentine (the adjective from Trent, derived from its Latin form) decrees, the theological initiative was almost completely in the hands of the Protestants. Catholicism had been subjected to a seemingly endless series of attacks with no coherent or positive response. All that there had been was a string of defensive statements that appeared to be little better than lame excuses. The morale of Catholics in most of Europe – Spain was the obvious exception – was generally very low, partly because it seemed to them that they were 'on the losing side'. The work of the Council significantly altered this state of affairs, and helped to generate a positive spirit among leading Catholics, most of whom could recognise that their side was now putting up a proper fight.

It would be convenient to be able to show that one of the short-term effects of the Council was to stem or even to reverse the tide of Protestant advance. Unfortunately the evidence does not justify this type of judgement. Nevertheless, the terminology often used to describe the dealings between Protestants and Catholics in the sixteenth century has tempted numbers of writers to go further than is supported by the facts. The talk has been of metaphorical warfare, made up of 'battles' and 'campaigns'. It has been very easy to identify 'turning points' within this military analogy. The Council of Trent has frequently been described as such a turning point. Unfortunately, it is not possible to establish a causal relationship between the Council and any Protestant reversals. The fact that the Council took place at a time when Protestant advances were slowing down, especially in Germany and Italy – although less obviously so in Britain and France – does not prove that it was the cause of this general change in religious fortunes. In fact, although it is equally unprovable, it is probable that the work of the Jesuits and of the Inquisition had more direct effect on limiting or reversing the spread of Protestantism than did the decisions of the Council of Trent.

* Short-term effects are frequently long-term effects in a slightly different guise. The Council had both a short-term and a long-term effect on the position of the Papacy. Both effects were in the same direction. Before the Council met there was a distinct possibility that the policies of the conciliarists would triumph and that the Pope would be confirmed as the figure-head of the Church, but with effective power residing with an internationally-selected representative body. The paradox was that the Council of Trent effectively resolved the issue in the Pope's favour without ever dealing with the matter in a formal manner. Attempts were made, especially in the early months and during the final period, to challenge the Pope's position, but they were skilfully deflected by the Legates, who were then able to confirm the Pope as effective head of the Church by ensuring that sensitive issues on which the Council could not agree were referred to him for decision. It was, of course, the Pope who made the Council's decrees official by conferring his blessing on them, as Pius IV did in their entirety in 1564. In the short-term the Pope's position was strengthened as he became the unchallenged head of the Church. The hierarchical nature of the Church had been accepted when it was agreed that only the Pope could appoint a bishop, just as it was decided that only bishops could appoint parish clergy. And in the long-term the Catholic Church was secure as a highly centralised Italian ecclesiastical monarchy. It was not mere coincidence that no Pope for more than three centuries felt the need to summon a further general council, or that no Pope for more than four centuries was non-Italian.

* There is little doubt that the Council of Trent had several long-term effects on the nature of Catholicism. Although much radical and challenging theological thinking had been undertaken by Protestants in the decades before Trent, there had been many parallel, but less publicised, strands of development within the Catholic Church. The decisions made at Trent put an end to most of this. As long as much of the detail of Catholic dogma had remained undefined it had been possible for there to be lively debate between theologians within the Church, as the parameters of what was acceptable were widely drawn. But once there were clear cut statements of the Church's teaching on most of the contentious issues, the room for discussion was much reduced. Loyal acceptance was what was demanded of Catholics. What is more, the fact that the dogma adopted by the Council was generally conservative meant that the teachings of the Church were settled in a reactionary mould for centuries to come. For the next 400 years, the popular perception could safely be that innovation and the Catholic Church were opposites.

Not only did the Council of Trent force Catholicism into a conservative mould, it also determined the nature of its spirituality. While Protestants became a group of reflective Bible readers, tending towards simplicity in corporate worship and richness in private contemplation, Catholics were ushered away from the Bible towards the writings of the saints and the fathers of the Church, and tended towards colourful and dramatic church services in which the stimuli of sight and sound were more important than the engagement of the conscious mind. The twin emphases of ecclesiastical tradition as a source of religious truth, and the efficacy of good works led Catholic practices in an opposite direction to those of the Protestants and ensured that the gap between them would widen rather than narrow over time. Whereas public individual spirituality, such as extempore (spontaneous) prayer and statements of personal faith, became commonplace among many Protestant groups, the Catholic who approached his religion too thoughtfully was often the focus of official suspicion.

This relatively low expectation of the spirituality of the ordinary Catholic was indirectly confirmed by the Council of Trent in the emphasis it placed on the separateness of the priesthood. This, of course, was in direct contrast to Protestantism with its common belief in 'the priesthood of all believers'. The Tridentine decrees defined the ways in which 'merit' could be acquired by the individual believer. Most of these required the mediation of a priest, especially through the exercise of the sacraments of baptism, the Eucharist, confession and penance, and extreme unction when on the point of death. The individual Catholic was, therefore, spiritually helpless without the assistance of priestly members of the Church hierarchy. This, in time, led to the growth of clericalism (the social and political prominence of all levels of priest) within Catholic communities. Clericalism in turn gave rise to the anti-clericalism that, especially since the late eighteenth century, has been a marked feature of political life throughout the Catholic world. This rigid dichotomy was to have a dramatic effect on the later histories of France, Italy and Spain, in particular.

However, it should be recognised that it is frequently dangerous to make detailed claims about the long-term effects of an event. Although it is obvious that normal tests of proof do not exist in such speculations – for instance, it is not possible to prove that if the Council of Trent had not done what it did the Papacy would never have established a position of unchallenged leadership in the Catholic Church – it is always possible to maintain that other events were just as influential. It could, for example, be argued that the actions of the Jesuits or of the Popes themselves were just as responsible for the prominence of the Papacy as were the decrees of the Council of Trent. However, as long as it is remembered that discussions of long-term effects have to do with reasoned opinions and likelihood rather than with proof and certainty, they are a useful way of creating comprehensible patterns of the past. Certainly it is not reasonable to expect to find too many clearly documented causal relationships when discussing the significance of the

Council of Trent. Often the historian has to be satisfied with indicators that appear to point in a particular direction. This, of course, leaves the way wide open for the development of large numbers of contrary interpretations.

★ But even within this area of uncertainty some conclusions remain effectively unchallenged. For instance, it is known that the Council had very little short-term effect on Church discipline. The decrees only applied automatically within the Papal States. Before they could be put into effect elsewhere they had to be accepted by the governments of individual states. With a few exceptions, such as Poland and Portugal, where acceptance was almost immediate, this only happened slowly or partially. Although Philip II (the son of Charles V) speedily agreed to implement the Tridentine decrees within his territories of Spain, the Netherlands, portions of Italy and the overseas empire, it was with the reservation that his powers should in no way be diminished. As a result, no reforming action could be taken in Spanish lands without the King's explicit permission, which was often difficult to obtain. Meanwhile, French kings steadfastly refused to recognise the validity of the decrees and continued to make appointments to senior Church positions for purely political reasons right up to the Revolution. In 1615 the French bishops did agree to implement the decrees as far as they affected their own behaviour, but as there were no 'teeth' to this statement of good intentions, its effect was limited and patchy. A somewhat similar situation developed in Germany where, although the Imperial Diet consistently refused to recognise the decrees, many individual rulers chose to do so. But even where the government supported Tridentine policies, it required an energetic and determined bishop to utilise the powers conferred on him in order to overcome the resistance of those who had much to lose from the new policies – on pluralism and absenteeism in particular. Such people remained in short supply for several generations. Although no wide-ranging research has been undertaken to provide reliable statistical data on the pace of change, the limited information that has been gathered suggests that for a long time little changed in many areas. Even in Italy, where progress might have been expected to be speedy, it is perhaps surprising to find that in 1630 fewer than half the dioceses could boast a seminary.

However, there were many exceptions to the rule. The most spectacular of these was Carlo Borromeo (1538–85). Borromeo was the nephew of Pius IV and, acting as his private secretary, was responsible for maintaining the close working relationship with Cardinal Morone during the third period of the Council. In 1565 he was appointed Archbishop of Milan – the most important city in northern Italy – then under Spanish control. He was the first archbishop to reside in the city for more than a century. He devoted the last 20 years of his life to carrying out the duties of the bishop as specified by the Tridentine decrees. He imposed a rigid discipline on the churchmen within his jurisdiction, and he built up the provision for the training of new priests to such an extent that Milan served the priestly needs of Catholic Switzerland in much the same way as Geneva provided France with a large number of Huguenot (French Protestant) ministers. Because he was stubborn and inflexible he was regularly in dispute with the secular authorities of the city, and it was often left to the Pope and the King of Spain, personally, to sort out the difficulties. His struggles not only showed what was possible, but also illustrated the determination that was required for substantial progress to be made.

Although Borromeo was outstanding, he was not unique. There were dozens of bishops like him, especially in Spain, over the next century. As a result, the number of properly trained priests greatly increased, with very noticeable effect, especially when the work of the Jesuit colleges is also taken into account (see page 82). However, there were many more bishops who did not even pay lip service to the Tridentine decrees. Progress was very patchy. Yet a definite shift in direction was noticeable. Instead of dedicated churchmen being regarded as oddities, they were increasingly accepted as the norm after Trent. Perhaps the most significant effect of the Council in matters of discipline was the way in which it changed popular expectations of priests, bishops and the Pope. A clear ideal had been established, and the clergy could be encouraged to live up to it. Over the centuries an increasing number chose to do so.

Making notes on 'The Council of Trent'

As the Council of Trent is one of the topics on which you must be prepared to answer a complete question at A-level, your notes should be sufficiently full to provide you with enough material (facts and ideas) to do so. You should, therefore, make a more detailed record than you have for previous chapters. The chapter falls into three main parts:

1. Before the Council opened (sections 1 and 2) – this is background and only needs to be noted in outline.
2. The work of the Council (sections 3, 4, and 5) – this is central and should be noted in detail.
3. An assessment of the significance of the Council (section 6) – this requires most reflection before you write. Your notes should be a record of your thoughts about the analysis presented in section 6.

The following headings, sub-headings and questions should help you:

1. Background.

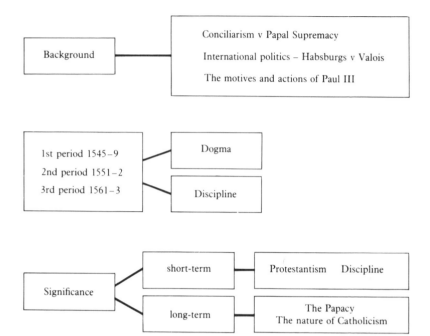

Summary – The Council of Trent

1.1. Why was the convening of a general council a contentious issue in the early sixteenth century?

1.2. Why did no general council meet in the early decades of the sixteenth century?

2.   Paul III.

2.1. Why did Paul favour the summoning of a general council?

2.2. What political difficulties faced Paul III in arranging for a general council to meet?

2.3. Venue.

2.4. Voting arrangements.

2.5. What steps did Paul III take to ensure that the initiative at a council would remain with the Papacy?

3.   The Pattern of the Council.

3.1. What was the pattern?

3.2. Why was this the pattern?

4.   The Teachings of the Church.

4.1. In what ways did the definition of dogma at the Council justify the term 'Counter Reformation'?

4.2. Sources of truth.

4.3. Interpretation of the Bible.

Answering essay questions on 'The Council of Trent'

Just because an essay question contains the words 'Council of Trent', it does not mean that it is restricted to this issue. Sometimes the question requires you to discuss the relative significance of the Council within the whole topic. Sometimes, of course, the question asks you to concentrate on only one aspect of the Council.

Divide the following questions into three groups. In the first group include the questions that require an overview consideration of the Counter Reformation. In the second group place the questions that deal with the Council in its entirety, and in the third group put the questions that concentrate on limited aspects of the Council.

1. 'Do you agree with the statement that "it was the Council of Trent that made Roman Catholicism a dynamic religion"?'
2. 'Was it the Council of Trent rather than the Jesuits that stemmed the tide of Protestant advance?'
3. 'How successful was the Council of Trent?'
4. 'What were the obstacles to the implementation of the decrees of the Council of Trent?'
5. 'How far had the aims of the Council of Trent been achieved by 1600?'
6. 'Why was the Papacy so successful at the Council of Trent?'
7. '"The Council of Trent was far more than a declaration of war on the Protestants." Discuss.'
8. 'What was the significance of the Council of Trent within the Catholic Reformation?'

The process you have just been through is an important one, because once you have consciously defined the scope of a question you are less likely to fall into one of the traps that most frequently results in a needless loss of marks in examinations – either omitting to cover aspects of the topic about which you know, but which you think are not relevant to the question, or wasting time writing about issues that you are not asked to consider, and, therefore, for which no credit will be given.

Select one of the questions from your second group – question 7 will be most appropriate. Are all aspects of the Council equally relevant in answering this question? Which of the following are most relevant to the question: the chronology of the Council; the working methods of the Council; the aims of the Council; the achievements of the Council; the limitations of the Council? Which of these aspects could safely be omitted from your answer?

Source-based questions on 'The Council of Trent'

1 Sources of truth
Read the extracts from the Council's decree, given on pages 52 and 53, and answer the following questions:

a) In what ways is the dogma described in the two extracts at variance with Protestant teachings?

b) What are the implications of this dogma for the relationship between the Catholic Church and its members?

2 Salvation
Read the extracts from the Council's decree, given on pages 54–55, and answer the following questions:

a) What is the meaning of the phrase 'let him be anathema' with which each of the canons ends?

b) What is the meaning of 'justify' and 'justification' as used throughout the extracts?

c) In what ways do the extracts support the contention that the framers of the decree had anti-Protestant intentions?

d) What are the implications for indulgences of canon 30?

e) Where would you place these extracts on the *continuum* from general to specific? What does this imply for freedom of discussion within the Catholic Church?

3 The Eucharist
Read the extracts from the Council's decree, given on pages 56–7, and answer the following questions:

a) Which traditional Catholic teaching is confirmed in the first extract? Why was this teaching objected to by Protestants?

b) What practices is the second extract defending?

c) How far is it justified to claim that this extract encapsulates the essential difference between Protestantism and Catholicism?

CHAPTER 5

The Jesuits

1 Introduction

In 1540 the Society of Jesus was officially established. Its members were known as Jesuits. For the next 250 years it was the most controversial organisation in Europe. The Jesuits attracted distrust, loathing and even paranoia from their opponents, and adulation from their supporters. Almost everybody had an opinion about them, and most of these opinions were based on emotions rather than facts. Even historians writing about the Jesuits have found it difficult to break free of the prejudices they had formed before they began their researches on the subject. Books on the Jesuits contain more overtly biased statements than are to be found in almost any other category of modern historical writing. Therefore, the student's first task in beginning any reading on the subject is to attempt to discover the author's point of view.

Unfortunately, it is not just a matter of distinguishing between Catholic and Protestant authors. Large sections of the Catholic Establishment have traditionally been almost as hostile to the Jesuits as have been the extreme Protestants. Nor is it a situation in which the non-religious have no stance to take. Writers with a humanitarian or a liberal democratic background have been equally unsympathetic to the Society. Part of the purpose of this chapter is to explore the reasons for this deep and persistent strength of feeling about the Jesuits.

Whether historians and other commentators have regarded the Jesuits as a God-given blessing or as an unmitigated disaster, they have generally been united in their judgement that the Society of Jesus was immensely influential. Most writers about the Jesuits seem to assume that without them there would have been no lasting Counter Reformation and no lasting papal paramountcy within the Catholic Church. Some respected historians have gone so far as to give the clear impression that the Jesuits *were* the Counter Reformation. It will be for each reader to form an opinion on the extent to which the Jesuits deserved this reputation.

2 Origins – Ignatius Loyola (1491–1556)

If it had not been for Ignatius Loyola the Society of Jesus would not have existed, let alone survived. He was its originator and its first leader. His inspiration motivated the early Jesuits, and his techniques of winning support were adopted by most of his followers. His ideas on the structure and ordering of the Society were implemented and upheld almost in their entirety. He was in a real sense the father of the Jesuits. Catholics refer to him simply as St Ignatius.

Ignatius Loyola was born into a minor aristocratic family in the Basque region of northern Spain in 1491. As a child he acquired the pride, determination and confidence that befitted his position as a leader in a warlike community. There was never any doubt that his life would be lived as a soldier of Spain. However, all this changed in 1521 while he was at home recuperating from wounds received in battle. In a series of deeply religious experiences resulting from a detailed thinking and 'feeling' through of the life and sufferings of Jesus, he became convinced that God wished him to dedicate his life to helping others to acquire a similar spirituality.

Both his resolve and his ideas were developed during the next four years. He spent most of the first year in contemplation at Manresa, a famous Spanish religious centre where he was able to mix with and learn from others who had come to similar conclusions. Ignatius became convinced of many things. Underlying all his thinking was the certainty that God's purposes were to be implemented through His one Church, the Catholic Church, and its one leader, the Pope. As far as his own future was concerned, he became certain that his mission was to convert the Muslim inhabitants of the Holy Land (Palestine), in which Jesus had lived his life on earth. But when, during his pilgrimage to Jerusalem in 1523, he failed to win support from any of the Christian groups working there, he concluded that God required him to become educated before he proceeded with his missionary work. He had been trained as a warrior from an early age, and therefore had received no formal education. As a result, he knew no Latin, the language of European learning. In order to overcome this deficiency he conquered his pride, and as a man of thirty-four joined a class of young boys to learn the rudiments of the language. He applied himself to his studies with such determination that within three years he had made sufficient progress to be able to cope with the demands of being a student at the University of Paris, the most prestigious centre of learning in the Catholic world.

During the seven years he spent in Paris, Ignatius gained not only a mastery of Latin but also a deep knowledge and understanding of the sacred Christian writings of the previous 1,000 years. These enshrined most of the traditions in which theologians were steeped. At the same time he built up a small band of friends and followers who became totally committed to his ideas, aspirations and arguments. In 1534 seven of them took a common vow to dedicate their lives to God by working in the world, rather than by withdrawing from it, as monks did. In particular, they vowed to undertake missionary work in the Holy Land. Recognising that this might not be practicable because of the difficulty of crossing the Mediterranean at a time when the Ottomans and the Venetians were at war, they committed themselves to undertake whatever work the Pope might assign to them should their first preference be unattainable. They agreed to assemble at Venice in

1537 in readiness for embarkation to Palestine.

After a year of waiting in Venice for the international political situation to become more settled, they had to admit to themselves that they were not going to be able to carry out their original intention. But the time had not been wasted. They had established a reputation in Venice as a group of remarkable men whose utterly selfless dedication to the sick and the poor was outstanding. They appeared to be living saints. Nobody could reasonably interpret their motives as containing any element of self-interest. During their time of waiting in Venice they had been joined by three further 'brothers', making ten in total, and they had all been ordained as priests. They continued their good works as they made their way south in pairs to offer their services personally to the Pope. In the highly politicised atmosphere of Rome, the arrival of an international (five Spanish, two French, two Savoyard and one Portuguese) band of poverty-stricken and naive 'do-gooders' made no immediate impact. However, even in the Eternal City where worldly wisdom was the norm, the contribution being made by Loyola and his companions was favourably noticed in time. Their complete commitment to the welfare of others, with seemingly no thought to their own health or comfort, gained them friends in high places. Through the intercession of those close to the Pope, Paul III agreed to their establishment as the Society of Jesus in 1540. What was envisaged by Paul was a small brotherhood of up to 60 dedicated men who would carry out charitable works wherever and however he directed them. It was not imagined that this new organisation would be of more than very limited local significance.

How was it, then, that the Jesuits so quickly became a major influence within the Catholic Church?

3 Jesuit Methodology

One of the features that marked out the Society of Jesus from the many similar groups that emerged in Catholic communities during the first half of the sixteenth century was its possession of a powerful strategy for winning support. This was a programme of activity carried out by a single Jesuit with a single 'client'. It had been devised by Ignatius Loyola and was modelled closely on the experiences he had gone through during his spiritual awakening at Manresa. It was known as the *Spiritual Exercises*. Loyola had been through the programme with each of his followers as part of their entry to the group. At the heart of the *Spiritual Exercises* was an extended period, ideally of several weeks, of retreat from the world during which a planned sequence of contemplations on the life of Jesus took place. The contemplations, which involved imaginative reconstructions of the events of Jesus's life, and an attempt to experience what were thought to have been his feelings, were interspersed with sessions during which the client committed himself or herself to live a more Christ-like life.

Not only those intending to join the Jesuits followed the *Spiritual Exercises*. Anybody who was felt to be seriously seeking spiritual growth could be taken through the programme if they could find a Jesuit prepared to devote sufficient time to them. For most people the effect of following the *Spritiual Exercises* was to release a flood of spiritual energy and to engender a feeling of inner well-being. As a result, it was very rare for a client not to become a fervent supporter of the Society, even though most of them did not become members. Because it quickly became a mark of social distinction to have undertaken the *Spiritual Exercises*, the rich and famous throughout Catholic Europe were soon clamouring for an opportunity to undergo this new dramatic experience. As a result, many kings, princes, other rulers, and their wives, became committed Jesuit supporters during the 1540s. In part this was because Loyola consciously targeted his efforts on those with influence, knowing that rulers who were pledged to Catholicism were the surest antidote to the spread of Protestantism. But it was also because he was not in a strong position to resist the persistent demands of members of the social élite, who were quick to go behind his back, if need be, to persuade the Pope to order that a Jesuit be assigned to them. The net result was that by 1550 there was hardly a Catholic state, however small, in which at least one of the leading figures was not a Jesuit sympathiser. In many states, especially in southern Germany and Italy, it was the ruler who was the source of Jesuit support.

One of the strengths of the *Spiritual Exercises* was their infinite flexibility. There was no standard formula. Although the published edition achieved widespread circulation in southern Europe, it was in no sense a self-instruction manual. Without careful guidance the publication was largely meaningless. What made the *Spiritual Exercises* so influential was the ready availability of well-trained guides to accompany clients through their spiritual journeys. Part of the skill of the guide was in assessing the spiritual needs and abilities of each client, and in tailoring the exercises accordingly. Some clients were not, and never would be, ready to undertake the full programme. But it did not mean that they were denied the opportunity to derive what benefit they could from it. What was important in Loyola's eyes was that each client felt spiritually enriched as a result of the experience, and was committed to some improvement in future conduct. He readily accepted that, for the very sinful, there might still be a long way to go.

The uses to which the *Spiritual Exercises* were put has brought much criticism of the Jesuits over the centuries. Protestants, in particular, have accused the Jesuits of undertaking what nowadays would be termed 'brainwashing'. Calvinist pamphleteers rejoiced in likening Jesuits to devil-workers and in portraying their clients as innocent victims whose freedom to make their own decisions had been stolen from them. In the sixteenth and seventeenth centuries, when belief in witches and other agents of the Devil was widespread, this was a powerful argument for hostile propagandists to present. Equally frequently, the Jesuits were accused of being hypocrites and self-seekers. They were taunted with only being interested in those who were politically powerful, and with allowing their influential supporters to carry on sinning without correction. This was not a surprising line of attack as some of the most famous Jesuit supporters were well known for their extreme immorality, even after they had been through the *Spiritual Exercises*. Even a well disposed public could not understand why the Jesuits continued to give a ruler personal spiritual support after his continuing sinfulness had become common knowledge. It was lame and unconvincing for a Jesuit to justify himself by claiming that his client was doing the best he could, and that to withdraw the support would probably worsen the situation. It is, therefore, probably fair to describe most of the early Jesuits as pragmatists. But there is no evidence that more than the occasional member was self-seeking or hypocritical.

* The tact and flexibility shown by Jesuits in their dealings with the rich and the powerful was a major factor in their rapid rise in prominence. They realised that to be influential they first had to be acceptable. This did not happen by chance. Loyola frequently gave his followers written advice on how they should act in this respect:

1 In conversing with persons of rank or power consider first, in order to win their affection for the greater service of God Our Lord, of what temperament they are and adapt yourselves thereto . . . In all speech with others by which we desire to win them and
5 put them in the net for the greater service of God Our Lord, let us follow the method adopted by our enemy, the devil, in his dealings with a good man . . . He goes in by the other man's door to come out by his own, not contradicting but approving his habits . . . In like manner, we, for our good purpose, may
10 applaud or agree with another in regard to some matter in itself innocent, passing over other things of a bad complexion, so as to win his sympathy and further our good purpose . . . In all dealings with others, especially when acting as peace-makers or giving spiritual advice, it is necessary to be guarded, remember-
15 ing that everything one says may or will become public.

A similar approach was adopted in most dealings with Protestants, where the aim was clearly to secure their conversion. This was in marked, and readily noticeable contrast to the way in which Protestants normally acted towards Catholics, where the tradition of communicating loathing and hatred, begun by Martin Luther, was strongly established. Loyola wrote:

1 . . . whoever desires to become useful to the heretics of this age
   must be solicitous to bear them much charity and to love them
   truly, excluding from his mind all thoughts which tend to cool his
   esteem for them. Secondly, it is necessary to gain their good will,
5 so that they may love us and keep a place for us in their hearts.
   This we can achieve by familiar intercourse with them, speaking
   of the things which we have in common and avoiding all
   contentious argument.

However, it should not be thought that the Jesuits were in any sense irresolute. They could be extremely flexible about the means they adopted but they were not prepared to negotiate over ends. They were among the most intransigent of Catholics. In the 1540s when there was still widespread hope of agreement being reached with the Protestants of Germany, the Jesuits were convinced that the only way forward was for the Lutherans either to rejoin the Catholic Church or to be destroyed. Equally they were totally unprepared to compromise on any matter of faith, including the primacy of the Pope as head of the Church. It was this steadfastness and determination that made the Jesuits so popular in Rome in the 1540s, when the earlier reforming drive within the Church, aimed at meeting the Protestants half way, had been replaced by a determination to reform Church discipline while insisting on uniformity of doctrine. This approach eliminated all possibility of reaching agreement with heretics. Popes saw the Jesuits as able and totally reliable allies.

The perceived ability of the Jesuits was partly the result of the standing of some of its leading members as theologians. Although Ignatius Loyola was not academically brilliant, several of the founding members of the Society were. Lainez, who succeeded Loyola as General of the Society, and Salmeron were so well thought of in this respect that they were used extensively by Popes as official theologians at the Council of Trent. Their uncompromising but erudite contributions at the Council did much to establish an international reputation for the Jesuits as leading spokesmen for orthodoxy. Over the decades this reputation was confirmed as the Jesuits managed to recruit and train some of the most able Catholics of the period. There was a consciously formulated policy, begun by Loyola and continued by his successors, of devoting considerable energy to educating Jesuits to the highest level of which they were capable. This resulted in the production of a steady stream of able theologians who were well-equipped to meet the Protestant doctrinal challenge.

4 Jesuit Organisation

The prominence of the Jesuits was to a significant extent due to the structure and organisation of the Society. It was the rules that governed the Society and the way in which they were implemented that marked out the Jesuits as being different from the other small groupings of priests founded at about the same time. The Society's rules, known as the Constitutions, were formulated in detail by Loyola and his closest associates between 1547 and 1551, although they had existed in a more generalised form since the late 1530s. They were accepted by the voting members of the Society and endorsed by the Pope. They confirmed the status of the Society as a spiritually élitist organisation.

The Constitutions specified in great detail how entry to the Society was to be gained. These all-embracing regulations made it possible for large numbers of boys and men to commence the process of securing membership of the Society. But the length and the severity of the induction programme ensured that it was very difficult to achieve full membership. Almost all religious orders stipulated that newcomers should enter a period of novitiate, during which their fitness to undertake their expected future duties could be assessed. A novitiate normally lasted for one year, after which successful novices would enter fully into the order. The Jesuit Constitutions specified a much more demanding process. Novices undertook an initial two-year probation, during which their spiritual ardour was tested when they were required to carry out menial tasks for the benefit of the most underprivileged, often in hospitals or prisons. Most novices were required to undertake a pilgrimage, barefoot and relying on begging for their sustenance. Those who survived this initial period of service entered the Society at the lowest level and began a programme of education of unspecified duration. When education was considered complete, sometimes after as long as a decade, the Jesuit-in-training was ordained a priest and began the third stage of his induction. This was a year-long second novitiate during which spiritual strength was tested under the close scrutiny of a superior. If all was to the required standard at the end of this stage, formal entry to the Society would take place. Even then there would be careful selection. Most entrants were 'solemnly professed', meaning that they retained the possibility of progressing to the highest level in the Society. The remainder became 'spiritual co-adjators'. This was the lowest rank of priestly brother, and indicated that the person was not thought capable of intellectually demanding duties. Only outstanding recruits were invited, then or at any time, to add a fourth vow to their earlier promises of poverty, chastity and obedience. This was the vow to go wherever the Pope chose to send them, and marked out the leading members of the Society. To become a fully professed member, as those who had been allowed to take the fourth vow were termed, was regarded as a signal honour. It conferred voting membership of the

Society's General Congregation – the body that elected the Society's leader and agreed all major changes of policy. In 1556 there were about 1,000 Jesuits, most of whom were in training. There were only 43 fully professed members.

The academic and spiritual élitism of the fully professed members of the Society did not mean that there was no place for those who were not intellectually able. Although Loyola's clear intention was to restrict full membership to the outstanding few, it was quickly found that there were obvious benefits in allowing highly committed but non-studious recruits to play some part in the Society. In the early years of explosive growth for the Jesuits, when the demand for their services far outstripped the supply of brothers, there was every reason to recruit ardent supporters whose abilities fitted them for behind-the-scenes roles within the organisation. So an additional grade of brother was allowed – that of lay-brother. Lay-brothers were not ordained as priests, nor did they receive any formal education. Their major role was to attend to the physical needs of their fellow brothers, typically by acting as companions for them on difficult journeys or by cooking for them when resident. But they were much more than servants. They played a full part in the spiritual activities of their communities and they were not marked out as menials. All brothers spent a proportion of their time carrying out duties of the most lowly kind. These were not reserved for the lay-brothers.

The Jesuits were marked out by their efficiency. The Society has often been likened to a military organisation. This parallel has been encouraged by the stress that was placed on obedience within the order, although the fact that the leader was known as the General was of no significance. It was also justified by the way in which nearly all decisions about the deployment of human and other resources were taken in Rome, even when members of the Society were distributed throughout the known world. Given the standards of the time, when the unreliability of communications and the lack of a well-developed bureaucracy meant that centralised control of any operation was extremely difficult, the achievement was remarkable. It was attained because of the immense administrative dedication of Loyola and the handful of assistants he gathered around him. Between them they produced thousands of lengthy hand-written letters per year, each produced in multiple copies and sent by various routes in the hope that at least one copy would reach its destination. These letters were essential if the degree of control aspired to by Loyola was to be exercised from the centre.

It was equally important to ensure a regular flow of information to Rome from the regions. Without a detailed knowledge of what was happening to Jesuits elsewhere, the General could not offer appropriate advice and instructions. The regular reporting to Rome of everything of significance that happened to the brothers in their work was rapidly established as an obligatory practice within the order. A huge number of these letters has survived, allowing historians to build up detailed pictures of events as perceived by the Jesuits. However, the relative paucity of records relating to the same events from other sources has possibly tempted some historians to exaggerate the significance of the actions of the Jesuits. It may be that some part of the supposed historical significance of the Jesuits is merely a consequence of the survival of a large amount of documentary evidence about their activities.

Yet the temptation to regard the Jesuits as a highly organised, multi-national army of the Counter Reformation should be resisted. Protestant propagandists regularly attempted to portray them as sinister subverters of spiritual independence, working according to a closely co-ordinated master plan. But the propagandists' clear aim was to spread fear and distrust of the Jesuits. They were not interested in establishing the truth. They had only to ensure that there was sufficient credibility to their claims for their exaggerations to be believed by those who were already inclined to do so. Detailed study of the surviving Jesuit records shows how infrequently Loyola's ideal was carried out in practice. Some leading Jesuits, who were placed in authority over their brothers as Provincials in charge of a Jesuit province – which could be as large as China and Japan combined, or as small as half of Spain – were effectively uncontrollable. While they claimed the intention of being obedient, they often made every excuse to avoid implementing policies with which they disagreed. This was particularly so with Provincials in Spain and Portugal, who regularly sheltered behind the supposed wishes of their monarchs in order to avoid carrying out the instructions of their General. Even the sending of a Vicar-General, conferred with overriding powers from Rome rarely made any difference. This was because the Society of Jesus did not employ the methods of a twentieth century police state in exercising control over its members. Reason and persuasion, coupled with unending patience, typified the approach adopted. This policy was initiated by Loyola and was continued by his successors. It was carried out at all levels of leadership and was typified by the constant praise of virtue and the gentle admonition of faults. Superiors were urged by Loyola to treat their men with kindness and consideration. In this he led by example. Many commentators have seen this approach to discipline as one of the most endearing aspects of the Society. But it can not be claimed that it helped the Society to function as a well-oiled machine, carrying out the orders of the Pope and its General without question.

Nevertheless, although the sixteenth century Jesuits were in no sense the efficient international conspirators that they have often been portrayed as being, they presented a remarkably united and coherent public image. They were far in advance of any other Catholic organisation of the time. The consistent stance of the Jesuits was easily maintained by the fact that the General of the Society was elected for life and not for a short period as was the case with almost every other leader of a religious order within the Catholic Church. This aspect of the constitutional life of the Jesuits removed one of the major potential causes of political in-fighting within the order. Other orders often suffered considerable distraction as a result of the constitutional need to elect a new leader every few years. This concern was removed from the Jesuits by the wording of their Constitutions, but they were almost forced to relinquish election for life by Pope Paul IV who showed considerable hostility towards the Society. His verbal instruction that a new General should be elected every three years was judged by lawyers to be binding only during the Pope's lifetime. It was therefore ignored after his death.

The Constitutions were highly effective in ensuring that the Jesuits were not deflected from their intended purposes. Their aim was to live completely in the world, and not to be partly withdrawn from it, as was the custom with most other religious orders. Partial withdrawal into exclusive community life was traditionally thought to be important in ensuring the salvation of the individual's soul. It was also seen as a vital component in securing effective discipline within an order. The normal way of meeting this requirement was for all members to live together and to devote part of each day to the communal celebration of mass. Loyola was determined that his order should not be constrained in this manner. His insistence attracted much adverse comment in high places. Paul IV's disapproval of the Society was partly caused by its lack of communal worship and he ordered that the Jesuits should fall into line with other orders. This was done during his lifetime, but Loyola's wishes were honoured once more after Paul's death. This made certain that Jesuits devoted nearly all their time and energy to what they regarded as being the worship of God through service to others. Loyola looked upon those who wished to devote significant amounts of time to contemplation and prayer as self-indulgent. Many letters were written admonishing brothers who frequently exceeded the hour per day that was allowed for such activities.

Attempts were made to avoid other potential distractions by specifically outlawing activities which either had brought other groups into disrepute or had acted as a drain on their resources. Loyola was not a woman-hater but he realised that even innocent contact with them in private could easily be misunderstood, as many friars had found to the cost of their reputations. Jesuits were therefore forbidden to act as confessors or spiritual advisers to groups of nuns, a stipulation that had the added advantage of protecting the brothers from some of the demands that were made on their time. Potentially more disruptive was the possibility that members of the Society would be used to fill ecclesiastical offices that were proving difficult to staff with men of an appropriate calibre. There was an established custom of using the services of leading friars in this way, to the obvious detriment of their orders. Loyola would have liked to forbid any Jesuit from accepting any office, but his obligations to the Pope prevented him from doing so. Therefore, he had to be content with a ruling that was a little less than absolute. But at least he was able to ensure that Jesuits would only accept office if specifically instructed to do so by the Pope. Fortunately for the Jesuits, successive Popes were prepared to honour the spirit of the Constitutions. Even when Ferdinand of Austria exerted consider-able pressure on Rome to allow a Jesuit to become Bishop of Vienna, he was only successful in obtaining a temporary appointment. So Jesuits were generally kept available to carry out the activities for which their order had been established.

5 Jesuit Activities

When the Society of Jesus was founded, it was expected that its major contribution to the Catholic Church would be in providing manpower for missionary work among infidels and heathens. For most of the men who aspired to become Jesuits during the first century of the Society's existence – and there were many thousands of them – this was the main motivating force. The most commonly expressed wish among them was to serve in foreign lands and to be martyred for their faith. The positive desire to die for Jesus was widespread, and not greatly to be wondered at, given the assumptions that most Jesuits shared. They looked upon life as a generally painful period of novitiate which was the necessary prelude to an eternity of contentment to be spent with God. They believed that their destiny was in God's hands and that he would call them to him (through death) when he was ready. They were certain that in the meantime it was their duty to give no thought to the satisfaction of their own desires, and to devote all their energies to living as Christ-like a life as possible. Many lapsed from this high ideal, but it seems that a high proportion of Jesuits frequently came close to meeting the expectations that were held of them.

A fine example was set by Francis Xavier, one of Loyola's original companions, who became the best known Christian missionary of modern times. He journeyed with Portuguese merchants in an attempt to bring news of Christianity to the lands of the mysterious East. He worked in the field, mainly in southern India and Japan, from 1542 until 1552 when sickness finally killed him. He was an extremist. He is greatly to be admired, or greatly to be pitied, depending upon the reader's system of values. He appears to have been almost completely unselfish, having trained himself to give no thought to his own welfare. He took totally unreasonable risks with his own health, and even his life, in the firm belief that God would protect him if that was His will. He gave virtually no thought to the practicality of his ventures. Once he had reached the destination of a journey he separated himself from all contact with Europeans, and launched himself on the local community with no knowledge of its languages and with no means of support. It was not surprising that he was judged by most of those he met to be a madman. But he managed to make contact with small numbers of people who were impressed by his obvious spirituality. He even made handfuls of converts to Christianity, although the extent to which most of them understood the implications of their commitment must be in doubt.

Although Xavier's influence on the lands he visited was minimal, the impact he had on Catholic Europe, and particularly on the Society of Jesus, was considerable. His exploits were known both from his own lengthy annual letters to Loyola and from the reports of those who knew of him. He was an inspiration to hundreds of young Jesuits who developed the wish to follow in his footsteps. He was living proof that the high ideals taught in the Jesuit colleges could really be put into practice. Over the next two centuries hundreds of Jesuits were allowed to offer themselves for missionary work of the type he had pioneered, although many more were refused permission because their services were required in Europe. Throughout the period of growing Portuguese and Spanish influence in Asia, Africa and the Americas, a steady flow of Jesuit missionaries left Iberian ports for the dangerous journey east or west. They concentrated on areas which were either recently discovered or with which contact had only recently been made. Many never reached their destinations, being shipwrecked and becoming yet further victims of the policy of European expansion. Many more survived for only a short time after their arrival at their intended destinations. They fell victim either to the uncomprehending savagery of the existing inhabitants or to the effects of disease and deprivation. But there were some startling if temporary successes in most unpromising situations, especially in the Portuguese areas of influence in India, Japan and East Africa. As in Europe, the key appeared to be the support, or at least the sympathetic tolerance, of local rulers. Many lives were lost and many years of patient suffering were endured in an effort to gain the patronage of important dignitaries. There were enough victories for it to be believed that the effort was not completely wasted, although there were times when Jesuit leaders seriously doubted the wisdom of committing more of their scarce resources to such unpromising ventures. But the Jesuit stress on missionary work remained, especially in the Society's Portuguese Province.

 * If the conversion of non-Christians was Loyola's initial motivation in founding his Society, it was closely followed by a genuine commitment to education. In the early years, the assumption was that Jesuit educational initiatives would be confined to the training of those who intended to join the Society. Colleges were quickly founded for this purpose. The most famous of these was in Rome, to which young men from all over Europe were attracted by the high academic and spiritual

reputations that were rapidly established. They were certainly not lured by any prospect of opulence or comfort. Loyola was determined to prevent the Society from becoming corrupted by riches. He frowned on the seeking and accepting of endowments, and although he was prepared to make exceptions in the case of Jesuit colleges, the popular image of Jesuits as people who wished to be poor seems to have discouraged most potential patrons. As a result, grinding poverty was normally the lot of those who taught and studied in the colleges. They were often expected to survive for long periods of time on bread and water, while spending their nights on crudely made beds in rooms that did not keep out the elements.

The colleges were intended to meet the complete educational needs of the Society. From the beginning the plan was to provide what would nowadays be described as both secondary and university education within each institution. Because there was so little provision of good quality secondary education, in Italy and southern Germany especially, the demand rapidly grew for the early Jesuit colleges to admit the sons of the local élite, even when there was no prospect of the boys entering the Society. There were equally pressing demands for new colleges to be established which would be open to the local population. Because much of the pressure was applied directly to the Pope, and because Popes were eager to please rulers where there would be no cost to themselves and no diminution of their powers, Loyola and his successors frequently found themselves in receipt of an instruction to found further colleges, despite the fact that their resources, especially of manpower, were already greatly overstretched. By 1556 there were over 100 Jesuit houses. Most of these were colleges catering for the education of both intending Jesuits and the sons of the well-to-do. This development came about by chance rather than by intention. But despite this, it was one of the major causes of the Society's long-term effectiveness. Even before the end of the century, many of the most influential political figures in Catholic Europe had received their education at the hands of the Jesuits. As the basis of that education was the instillation of both a love and a fear of God, and an acceptance of the teachings of the Catholic Church, including the primacy of the Pope, it can justly be claimed that the Jesuits did much to shape the politico-religious climate of late sixteenth and early seventeenth century Catholic Europe.

* Missionary work and educational work were the two most time-consuming activities for the Jesuits in the Counter Reformation period. Many more man-hours were spent on each of these tasks than on all other activities put together. But these were not the only duties of significance carried out by Jesuits. Popes used leading members of the Society as papal representatives on especially sensitive missions and at especially important meetings. This was particularly the case when local Catholic rulers were attempting to reach agreements with Protes-

tants. Lainez, while General, spent many months in France attempting to ensure that Catherine de Medici did not compromise the Catholic position in her negotiations with the Huguenots, and others had been given a similar role in Charles V's later conferences with the Lutherans. In the process the Jesuits earned themselves a reputation as wreckers of possible compromises and hypocrites who spoke words of friendship to their opponents and pretended to listen to their arguments, while already having made up their minds that no agreement must be reached. It was the beginning of the popular perception that it was dangerous ever to accept a Jesuit at face value.

Individual Jesuits were also used to establish a position of influence with key political figures on a long-term basis. To commit the total energy of one member to acting as the full-time confessor or spiritual director of only one 'client' was an expensive use of resources, but it was considered worthwhile if it proved effective in bolstering the resolve of a ruler or a leading minister to maintain the position of the Church within the state. At one time or another, by the end of the seventeenth century, there was significant Jesuit influence in the day-to-day running of nearly every Catholic state. The fact that the Jesuits concerned rarely occupied any official position, and did not publicly admit to the influence they exercised, allowed opponents to stir up fears about these shadowy *eminences grises* whose first loyalty appeared to be to the Pope rather than to the ruler they pretended to serve. The local political élites were quick to demand the expulsion of all Jesuits in such situations. They were sometimes successful, as in both France and Spain from time to time. The Pope was even persuaded to suppress the Society altogether for a period during the late eighteenth and early nineteenth centuries. But by then the Jesuits had completed their most telling work.

During the first 50 years of its existence the Society provided much of the manpower used by the Papacy in its efforts to reverse the spread of Protestantism in Europe. Jesuit missions were dispatched to France, Germany, England, Ireland, Scotland, Poland and Scandinavia, in some cases on numerous occasions and in secret. Unfortunately for the Catholic cause, intelligence gathering about the outlying regions of northern Europe was woefully inadequate in Rome, and much time, effort, and even human life was squandered in pursuing possibilities that never really existed. But, given the absence of any reliable methods of collecting international news, it is not surprising that the existence of the Catholic Mary first as queen in Calvinist Scotland, and then as heir apparent (even if a prisoner) in Protestant England, should have misled the papal authorities into believing that a situation existed which they could exploit. A similar lack of success resulted from the missions to the Protestant states of Germany and Scandinavia, although Jesuits did play a part in stemming the spread of Calvinism in Poland.

With the exception of sixteenth-century France, much greater success attended the Jesuit efforts to prevent the further loss of Catholic lands to the Protestant cause. The three major battlegrounds in the second half of the sixteenth century were France, the Netherlands and southern Germany. In France the Jesuits did not manage to establish an influential position until the seventeenth century. During the 30 years from the mid-1560s to the mid-1590s, when the fate of Catholicism in the country hung in the balance, they could only maintain a tentative foothold in Paris by masquerading under another name, and by denying a first responsibility to Rome. Such was the strength of the traditional French distaste for Papal interference in their affairs that the Jesuits were almost as disliked by the Gallican Church hierarchy as the Huguenots. The survival of the Catholic Church in France in the late sixteenth century, therefore, owed very little to the efforts of Loyola and his successors. However, they played a more significant part in the eventual triumph of Catholic orthodoxy during the reign of Louis XIV.

By 1580 a strong Jesuit presence had been established in the southern Netherlands (modern Belgium) thanks to the support of Philip II and the local Prince-Bishops. In particular, the area was used as a training ground for Catholic fugitives from Protestant lands, such as England, in the hope that they would be able to return and reconvert their countrymen to their ancient faith. In this they were largely unsuccessful, but they did play a part in restoring Catholic morale within the Low Countries (alongside the Capuchins). It is impossible to be certain of the effects of this work, but it seems likely that the consolidation of the Catholic position in the area made it easier for Spain to retain control of the southern Netherlands once the north had won virtual independence in 1609.

It was in Germany, however, that the effects of the Jesuits were most felt in the struggle between Catholicism and Protestantism.

6 The Jesuits in Germany

The orthodox view is that it was in Germany that the Jesuits achieved their most dramatic effects during the sixteenth century. Many historians have viewed Germany as the front line in a war between Protestantism and the Catholic Church, and as the theatre that saw the turning point in the struggle. The metaphor has been of a tide of spreading Protestantism being stemmed in southern Germany and even starting to be rolled back. The Jesuits have normally been seen as the leaders and major facilitators of this Catholic resurgence.

The name of Peter Canisius (1521–97) has often been accepted as synonymous with Jesuit activity within the Empire. Canisius, known to Catholic authors as St Peter since his canonisation in 1925, was born the son of the leading citizen of the small Dutch town of Nijmegen in 1521. His parents were devout Catholics and Peter grew up aspiring to live a

Christ-like life. He was a very intense and serious-minded boy – an obvious candidate for recruitment into an extremist organisation while a student at Cologne University. The presence of the charismatic Peter Favre, one of Loyola's original companions, in the city ensured that it was the Jesuits towards whom Canisius was attracted. By 1543 he had become the first 'German' Jesuit. After time spent in Rome and in helping to found a Jesuit college in Sicily, he was sent to Ingolstadt in Bavaria in 1549. His task was to establish the first Jesuit college in Germany.

For the next 31 years Canisius worked unceasingly to prevent what he considered to be the realistic possibility of the whole of Germany becoming Protestant. He had no doubt that such an outcome would be a victory for the Devil, and would spell doom for the souls of millions of his adopted fellow countrymen. With what appeared to be complete certainty and perfect humility, he continued to uphold the claims and teachings of the Catholic Church even in the most unpromising situations. As a result of dogged determination – in some situations described as obstinacy – he achieved most unlikely successes. When he left Germany in 1580 to spend the remaining 17 years of his life teaching and preaching in support of Catholicism in the Swiss canton of Fribourg, the survival of papal influence in the Empire was assured and the structures that were to facilitate the Catholic advances of the early seventeenth century were firmly in place.

 * The leading Jesuits, including Canisius, appear to have analysed the situation perceptively and to have developed an effective strategy for dealing with it. The German princes who had so far remained Catholic were seen to be the key. It was recognised that once a ruler openly became a Protestant, there was little hope of maintaining the Church within his territories. It was therefore essential to do everything possible to prevent Catholic rulers from taking the irrevocable step of formally abjuring their faith. Canisius was introduced to this strategy early in his adult life. Favre's major task in Cologne was to persuade the Elector-Archbishop that he should not follow his convictions and declare for Lutheranism. There were many occasions on which the outlook was very bleak, but the expected disaster was always averted. In later years Canisius spent many hours speaking, writing and travelling to rulers whose commitment to the Catholic Church was thought to be wavering.

Canisius's major success was with Ferdinand of Austria. Ferdinand was Charles V's brother and was Holy Roman Emperor from 1556 to 1564. There was never a realistic possibility that he would become a Protestant himself, but there was a danger that he would make concessions to the Lutherans for reasons of political expediency. One aspect of this situation was critical to the Catholic cause. Canisius was keenly aware of the major significance of the Protestant princes' attempts to persuade Ferdinand to change one of the terms of the Peace

St Peter Canisius

of Augsburg. The Peace of 1555 had been intended to settle the 'religious question' in Germany by agreeing that there should be only one religion in each state, and that it should be either Catholicism or Lutheranism depending on the preference of the ruler. But the Protestant princes were not content with the stipulation that this arrangement did not apply to church lands – those states ruled by Prince-Bishops and Prince-Archbishops. By the terms of the Peace these territories could be nothing but Catholic. If the ruler of one of them became a Protestant, he had to relinquish his position, his titles and his income, and a fresh ruler had to be chosen. The Protestants wanted the church lands to be treated in the same way as all other states. It is likely that Ferdinand would have given way to this demand as the price to be paid for gaining support against the Turks had not Canisius frequently and forcefully reminded him that to do so would be to endanger his immortal soul. Had the major church states become Protestant it is very likely that many of the remaining Catholic states in Germany would have quickly followed suit. It would have been particularly significant had one of the Elector-Archbishops become Protestant. Four of the seven Electors would then have been non-Catholic. The frightening prospect of a Lutheran as Holy Roman

Emperor would have become a near certainty. It seems probable that it was Canisius's influence that prevented this happening.

The other danger to the continuation of a Catholic as Holy Roman Emperor was the religious allegiance of the Archduke Maximilian, Ferdinand's son and heir, who had already been elected King of the Romans and was therefore Emperor-elect. Maximilian became a Protestant in all but name in 1554, under the influence of Johann Phauser, a coarse but dynamic preacher who possessed many of the attributes that had made Martin Luther such an effective propagandist. His jovial good humour was spontaneously attractive, while his caustic attacks caused most opponents to wither. Canisius was no match for him, and his efforts to influence Maximilian were effectively blocked. The mere mention of Canisius's name was enough to throw Maximilian into a rage. Canisius had, therefore, to work through Ferdinand. After much persuasion, Ferdinand agreed to threaten his son with disinheritance if he became a Protestant. This was enough to convince Maximilian that his future lay within the Catholic Church, and the danger was averted.

Canisius was less successful in persuading Catholic rulers to take firm action against Protestants within their own territories. This was not surprising as there was seemingly little to be gained and much to be lost by antagonising what was often a powerful minority within the state. The Duke of Bavaria was prevailed upon to act against some of his powerful Protestant subjects, but in Austria little was done. Canisius spent most of the 1550s in Vienna where he even had to tolerate the fact that many of his colleague professors at the University were, at best, suspect in their faith. However, he did not consider this to be of prime importance, as long as the door to Catholicism was kept open sufficiently for his longer-term plans to come to fruition.

* The Jesuits, along with many reforming Catholics, had been quick to recognise that the greatest threat to the continuation of Catholicism in the German speaking lands was the paucity and poor quality of parish priests, especially in rural areas. For example, when Canisius was sent to Vienna in 1552 he found that the alarmingly high number of 254 parishes in the neighbouring province were without a priest. What Catholic parish priests there were in Germany were generally in stark contrast to the Lutheran clergy, who were well-trained and positively committed. It was widely reported by Jesuits and Protestants alike that it was relatively rare to find a Catholic priest in a country parish who could conduct services correctly, let alone live the type of life that would be an inspiration to his community. It was no wonder that many Catholics fell easy prey to itinerant Protestant preachers of quality. In an effort to remedy this situation the Jesuits devoted much of their energies to the foundation and development of a large number of colleges at which boys and young men could be schooled in Latin and the Catholic faith, hopefully in preparation for further training for the priesthood. There were about 40 of these colleges, all staffed by Jesuits,

in the German speaking world by 1600. They were intended to produce a steady stream of committed Catholics ready to become defenders of the faith in whatever role God intended for them, but especially within the Church.

On the whole the colleges were well regarded and had no difficulty in attracting able pupils. However, they were not of uniformly high quality. Some, such as those at Cologne and Vienna were large and thriving, containing more than 1,000 students each by the end of the century, while others, such as those at Innsbruck and Wurzburg, remained small and insignificant, failing to establish a positive reputation within their localities. But the fact that local and national dignitaries, including the Emperor, were prepared to entrust their sons   ˙ to the Jesuits did more than enough to counteract the adverse publicity caused by the failures.

It is normally asserted by historians that the Jesuit colleges spearheaded the Counter Reformation in Germany. Certainly it was the availability of large numbers of well-trained and well-motivated priests that made it possible to capitalise on the support of leading princes, especially the Habsburgs, and to bring about a Catholic revival in much of southern Germany and the Rhineland. But more work needs to be done by historians in firmly establishing that the improvement in the quality of Catholic clergy was the result of the work of the Jesuits. Only then will it be possible to claim without qualification that a simple cause and effect relationship exists. In the meantime, however, it appears realistic to maintain that the work of the Jesuits almost certainly made possible the revival of Catholic fortunes in Germany. The only nagging doubt is that this may be a case of historians being misled by the balance of readily accessible evidence. The work of the Jesuits in Germany, as elsewhere, is very well-documented while that of other Catholic groups is not. Almost every significant action of every Jesuit was recorded in a letter or a report, most of which have subsequently been published. No doubt it was the existence of over 7,500 printed pages of Canisius's letters that, for instance, encouraged James Brodrick to extend his biography of the saint to over 850 pages! There may well have been a too easy acceptance by historians of the Jesuits' own assessment of their importance.

* The role that Canisius played in the foundation and development of many of the colleges has been very fully researched. He certainly did not need to spend time seeking locations for potential new colleges, as many proposals came uninvited from princes who wished to have a college in their territory. In fact, Canisius often tried to deflect such invitations, being aware that there were insufficient Jesuits available to staff further ventures successfully. But, too often for his peace of mind, he was required by his superiors to proceed with establishing a new college in order to avoid giving offence to a powerful supporter.

Canisius's skill was in turning possibilities into realities. Most proposers of colleges were quick to make promises but very slow to take the action needed to facilitate the development of the college. Buildings were sometimes non-existent, and, when available, were nearly always unsuitable. Funds to meet running costs were repeatedly delayed, and extreme privation was suffered by the brothers as a result. When Canisius arrived at Ingolstadt in 1549 to establish a college at the Duke of Bavaria's request, no prior preparations had been made. The Duke was so slow in carrying out his promises – leaving the Jesuits to function as part of the existing university – that Canisius was transferred to Vienna after three years in an effort to force the Duke into action. Even this was ineffective and it was many years before a separate Jesuit college became a reality at Ingolstadt. When the Jesuits were persuaded by the Archbishop of Cologne to take over the University of Dillingen in 1563, a long period of tribulation began as the brothers, starved of funds, attempted to create something with very little. The pleas made to the Archbishop for the promised financial support fell on very deaf ears as the Archbishop himself was forced to spend most of his time in Rome in order to escape his creditors.

Canisius showed his saintliness in dealing with the problems of the colleges, which fell largely on his shoulders as Provincial of the Upper German Province of the Jesuits. He never complained about the ways in which he was let down, nor of the additional work that the broken promises caused him. He merely prayed that God would support the backsliders. Despite the terrors of long journeys in the sixteenth century, he visited each of the colleges in his Province at least once every year in order to help resolve those difficulties that required his presence. At other times he maintained contact through lengthy and frequent correspondence. He displayed the utmost patience in dealing with squabbles that broke out between members of staff at the colleges, never apportioning blame, and always seeking ways in which the strengths of his fellow Jesuits could be best used and their weaknesses minimised. He led by example, and in the process contributed greatly to upholding the morale of men who otherwise might have deserted the cause under the strain of intense work and distressingly poor conditions.

Canisius was also used to counter the appeal of the Protestants by utilising his considerable abilities as a preacher. For seven years from 1559 he acted as the main pulpit spokesman in Augsburg Cathedral, preaching three or four major sermons per week. He established himself as the leading Catholic focus for resistance to continued Protestant expansion. It was said at the time that he was directly responsible through his sermons for converting hundreds of people from Lutheranism to Catholicism. It was clearly because of this great personal influence that in the 1560s he was the object of a concerted campaign of vilification from leading Protestant spokesmen.

Under instruction from his superiors, he was also busy with the pen.

He was asked to prepare a clear and readable summary of Catholic teachings and to compose catechisms at various levels from it, so that those responsible for the spiritual welfare of both adults and children would have good quality teaching material to use. It had been speedily recognised by the Jesuits that the Lutherans and the Calvinists had marked advantages in this area. Canisius worked with great determination to produce what was expected of him. In 1555 his summary, *Summa Doctrinae Christianae*, was published along with catechisms for the young and for adults. Within a few years they had been translated into 15 languages, and were in use throughout the Catholic world. Unfortunately Canisius was not an inspired writer, although he was accurate and thorough. His works provided clear statements, but did little to lift the spirit of the reader. However, they adequately filled an obvious gap, and played a part in ensuring that Catholics could more easily prepare their hearts and minds against Protestant attack. They were not masterpieces, but they were worthy contributions to the cause of counter reformation.

Canisius achieved most during the 1550s and early 1560s. His contribution was much less significant during the 30 years up to his death in 1597. Yet he was as important to the Counter Reformation for what he was as for what he did. His life showed the people of Germany that it was possible to be both a Catholic and a person of true godliness. Brodrick characterises him as having 'simplicity and sincerity so radiant that even the coarsest consciences must feel their glow'. He clearly put God first in everything. He accepted all his many reverses and misfortunes as gifts from God, even if he could not understand how they fitted into a general plan. He was totally obedient to his superiors as God's representatives on earth, even when it appeared that they were wrong. He comforted himself with the belief that the seeming mistake must be part of God's purpose. He was convinced of his own unworthiness and consistently sought the prayers of his friends to increase his merit in the eyes of God. His daily life was built around prayer. Every action was accompanied by some request to God. He even whispered a short prayer between each mouthful of food. The fact that his prayers were largely mechanical rather than displaying great spiritual insight suggests that his religion was of the head rather than of the heart. Possibly for this reason he was respected and admired rather than loved. His life was completely disciplined and completely dedicated to what he understood to be the work of God, but he lacked warmth. His system of values, especially as revealed in his letters, is alien to a modern materialistic audience, but it is very revealing of the sixteenth century Jesuit mentality. When answering a letter from his step-mother informing him of the death of his father, he wrote:

1 You must always try to carry your cross patiently. . . . It makes me glad to know that sufferings are your lot because they are

proof that your faithful husband, my father, has not forgotten
you, however much you may forget your own self. Patient
5 suffering brings the sufferer to all tranquillity and peace. It
prepares us to receive the highest graces, wipes out the stains on
our hearts, opens blind and sin-sealed eyes, preserves us from all
pride and vain-glory, delivers us from the terrible pains of
Purgatory, and makes us careful and solicitous about our salva-
10 tion . . . As to whether we have deserved our sufferings or not,
what does it matter? The great thing is to suffer well and
patiently.

These sentiments are not greatly admired by most people four centuries
later, but at the time they were a source of inspiration to the many who
were frequent sufferers of pain and anguish.

7 Assessment

There is a dangerous tendency among commentators to assume that
popularity equates to effectiveness and success, while unpopularity
signifies non-achievement and failure. The Jesuits have generally
received a poor press over the past four centuries. Few kind words have
been written and fewer supportive judgements have been made, except
by authors who are themselves members of the Society. But it would be
very mistaken to conclude from this that the Jesuits were inconsequen-
tial.

It would be equally unwise to accept at face value the claims made by
the Jesuits themselves or by their Protestant opponents. Jesuit historians without exception exhibit explicit prejudice in that, however
much they describe Jesuit actions 'warts and all', they begin by
assuming the correctness of the Jesuit position. They do not subject the
claims of success to any rigorous scrutiny. Protestant controversialists,
on the other hand, exhibit equal prejudice, from an opposite direction
but with identical effect. They tend to use the Jesuits as scapegoats,
blaming them for the failure of the Protestants to capitalise on their
early successes, and accusing them of using unfair but very effective
tactics. Little evidence has ever been produced to support the assertions
and no serious attempt to quantify the effectiveness of the Jesuits as a
counter reformation force has been made.

It is likely that the truth lies somewhere between the two positions.
Probability, as well as the British tendency to gravitate to the compromise position, suggests that this is so. However, caution should be
exercised when assessing the contribution made by the Jesuits to the
Counter Reformation. Qualifying adverbs such as 'probably' and
'possibly' need to be much in evidence. But as long as these are present,
it seems defensible to describe the Jesuits as 'the spearhead of the
Counter Reformation' – the people who turned the aspirations and

theories of the Catholic reformers into reality. Even if it is not possible to be precise about the number of people they influenced or the extent of their effective influence in each case, it is certainly valid to maintain that their effect was both very widespread and very significant. It would even be possible to construct a convincing case that without their work the Counter Reformation would have ground to a halt at an early stage.

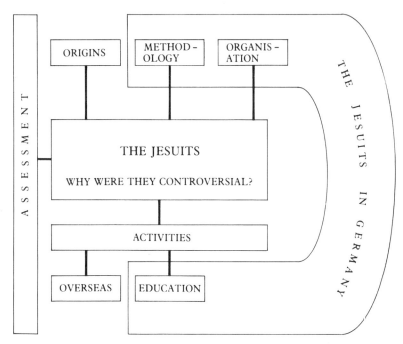

Summary – The Jesuits

Making notes on 'The Jesuits'

It is possible that you will be required to write an entire essay about the Jesuits. Therefore, your notes on this chapter should be full enough to allow you to prepare properly for this. The following headings, sub-headings, questions and suggestions should assist you in making your notes:

1.   Introduction. The issues that are central to the historical study of the Jesuits are identified in this section. Make a note of each of these issues in your own words.

2. Origins. Construct a date chart to include the events described in this section.
3. Jesuit Methodology.
3.1. The *Spiritual Exercises*. In what ways did these leave the Jesuits open to criticism?
3.2. Flexibility and intransigence. Over what were the Jesuits a) prepared and b) not prepared to compromise?
4. Jesuit Organisation. What were the strengths and weaknesses of the Jesuit organisation?
5. Jesuit Activities.
5.1. The overseas mission. Why have historians of the Counter Reformation paid relatively little attention to this aspect of their work?
5.2. Education. Why has this been regarded as being the Jesuits' most historically significant work?
5.3. Other activities. What were these, and of what importance were they?
6. The Jesuits in Germany. Use this section as a case study from which to compile a series of examples of Jesuit methodology, organisation and activities to be used as evidence to support the general points you have made in your notes on previous sections.
6.1. What were Peter Canisius's strengths and weaknesses?
7. Assessment. Write your own assessment of the relative significance of the Jesuits in the Counter Reformation. Make clear the provisional nature of your assessment, and the reasons for it being so.

Answering essay questions on 'The Jesuits'

Examiners have been fond of setting questions on the Jesuits, finding that the topic offers 'something for everyone'. Many of these questions have been about the Jesuits in general, but a significant minority of them have focused on Ignatius Loyola in particular. Yet you are unlikely to be expected to write for 45 minutes about Loyola alone. It is probable that you will be asked either to compare and contrast him with Martin Luther or John Calvin, or to assess his relative importance to the Counter Reformation. In the latter case you would be expected to devote a significant part of your answer to considering the significance of major events (such as the Council of Trent) and of other leading figures (such as Pope Paul III).

It will be worth your while, especially during the final weeks of revision, to think through the 'compare and contrast' question in respect of Loyola, Luther and Calvin. Into which aspects would you organise your analysis? You would certainly need to include some (if not necessarily all) of the following: aims; methods; character and personality; religious teachings; influence; strengths and weaknesses.

Sometimes such questions can appear deceptively simple. For example, the question 'Compare and contrast Martin Luther and Ignatius Loyola as religious leaders' is much more difficult than it seems, as no doubt you will find if you attempt to prepare a plan for answering it. It is essential to have thought through an analysis based on the aspects listed above before you begin to write. Otherwise you will not have clearly in mind the categories by which you are going to compare and contrast the two men, and you are almost certain to waffle!

Look at the following questions that include the word 'Jesuits':

1. 'How do you account for the success of the Jesuits in the sixteenth century?'
2. 'How influential were the Jesuits in the Counter Reformation?'
3. 'To what extent was the Catholic reform movement dependent on the Jesuits?'
4. 'What was the Jesuits' distinctive contribution to the Catholic Reformation?'
5. ' "The spearhead of the Counter Reformation." Is this an accurate description of the Jesuits?'
6. ' "The role of the Jesuits in the Counter Reformation was vital." Discuss.'

Three of these questions can be answered well by limiting your discussion to the Jesuits themselves. The other three questions require you to range over the whole topic of the Catholic and Counter Reformations. Decide on the category into which each question should be placed.

However, with all six questions you would be expected to devote more than half your time to considering the Jesuits, so do not be tempted to produce a pre-prepared answer on the Counter Reformation in general in such circumstances. You must also pay particular attention to the exact wording of the questions. For example, although questions 2 and 5 are asking essentially the same thing, they must be approached in different ways. One question demands a two-part 'in these ways and to this extent, yes / in these ways and to this extent, no' answer. Which question is this? What approach does the other question require?

Source-based questions on 'The Jesuits'

1 Jesuit methods
Study carefully the extracts from Ignatius Loyola's letters giving advice

on how to treat the powerful (page 75) and heretics (page 76). Answer the following questions:

a) Which group does Loyola most have in mind when he uses the term 'heretics' in the second extract?
b) What similarities does Loyola suggest in the treatment of heretics and the powerful?
c) What does Loyola hope the outcome of such treatment will be? Use quotations from both extracts in your answer.
d) Advice such as that given by Loyola led to the Jesuits becoming unpopular in many quarters. With whom were the Jesuits unpopular by 1600, and why?

2 Peter Canisius (1521–1597)

Study carefully the extract from Canisius's letter to his step-mother (pages 91–2) and examine the portrait of Canisius reproduced on page 87. Answer the following questions:

a) What does Canisius mean by 'carry your cross'? What is the implication of this metaphor?
b) What is Canisius's justification for advising his step-mother that 'the great thing is to suffer well and patiently'?
c) The portrait of Canisius is not from life, although it was probably based on contemporary material. In these circumstances, what aspects of Canisius is the artist attempting to communicate to the viewer? How is this done?
d) In what ways did Canisius's personality and attitudes, as suggested by the portrait and by the extract, particularly suit him to work in Germany at the time? Support your answer with details from your wider knowledge of Canisius's life.

CHAPTER 6

The Spirit of the Catholic Reformation

Most of those historians who champion the term 'Catholic Reformation' as opposed to the more traditional 'Counter Reformation' are not just arguing over words. They are asking for a change in the way in which the topic is perceived. They maintain that the changes taking place in the Catholic Church during the sixteenth century were essentially the result of a widespread spiritual awakening which had begun long before Martin Luther made his protest, and which would have re-shaped the Church even had Protestantism not emerged to provide the movement with a sense of urgency. They object to an analysis that typifies Catholicism as reacting to outside pressure rather than being revitalised from within. They have led the way in researching the lives of many of the notable men and women who exemplified the spiritual vitality which, for them, gave coherence to the history of sixteenth-century Catholicism. Their argument is that if only the actions of Popes, new orders, the Council of Trent and secular leaders are studied, the Catholic Reformation will not be properly understood. They claim that the vital spiritual dimension will be under-represented unless due prominence is given to the actions and attitudes of some of the leading exemplars of the revival within Catholicism. However, it must be accepted that it is impossible to make any realistic assessment of the influence of such people. It is clear that their example inspired many others to greater spirituality than they might otherwise have achieved, but because of obvious deficiencies in the written evidence, no meaningful quantification of this can be attempted. The study of their lives is an essential part of understanding the 'quality' rather than the 'quantity' of the Catholic Reformation.

1 John of the Cross (1542–91)

One of the complaints about the teachings of the Protestants made by many leading Catholics was that Luther and his followers denied people the opportunity to play a part in earning their own salvation. They maintained that the Protestant belief in salvation by faith alone was likely to discourage ordinary people from living moral and God-fearing lives, as the main incentive for doing so – the fear of damnation as the punishment for sin – had been removed. As a reaction to this aspect of Protestant teaching there was a clear emphasis within the Catholic Reformation on the performance of good works. Therefore, those Catholics who relied on contemplation and prayer rather than action (especially participation in the Church's sacraments) as a means of salvation became increasingly unpopular within the Church. They were even suspected of harbouring Protestant sympathies.

Yet there was a very strong tradition of religious contemplation within the Catholic Church, stretching far back into the early Middle Ages. Spain had a particularly rich inheritance of this mystical experience. As a result, there were hundreds of Spanish monks and nuns in the mid-sixteenth century who were in danger of being at odds with the direction in which their Church was moving. They lived lives aimed at achieving the ultimate goal of mystics – the unification of their souls with God by emptying their minds of all thoughts and desires other than of Him. One of the most influential of the Spanish mystics of the Catholic Reformation was Juan de Yepes (1542–91), known as John of the Cross.

Mysticism has received relatively little attention from British historians. They have generally found its concepts difficult to penetrate, and even more difficult to explain to those with limited religious experience. In addition, the values of the mystic have frequently been viewed as irrelevant in our largely materialistic society. Sometimes the historical significance of mysticism has been ignored because students have rejected its claims almost before they have been considered. However, the tradition deserves to be taken more seriously than this.

At the heart of mysticism is the belief that a state of spiritual perfection can be achieved by contemplation. This is almost always associated with a rejection of physical pleasures and desires. Mystics aim to concentrate all their attention on thinking about God and to spend as little time and energy as possible in meeting their own physical needs. An integral part of mysticism is asceticism. Determined ascetics deny themselves all unnecessary material comforts. They eat only enough to keep themselves alive, they occupy only the most rudimentary of shelters, and they possess no property other than the clothes they stand up in. Very often they punish themselves with extended fasting, by scourging their bodies, and by seeking out the most uncomfortable conditions under which to live. They do not do these things as ends in themselves, but in order to punish themselves for their sins and to further the process of eliminating their physical desires and their fear of pain. Their aim is to learn to suffer anything for God's sake.

John of the Cross was greatly influenced by these traditions as a child in Castile. By the time he had reached the end of his university education and had become a priest, he had already decided that his life must be lived as an attempt to secure unification of his soul with God. He was determined to follow the path of the mystic and the ascetic. But he had become a Carmelite friar two years previously and this was an obstacle. The rule under which he had vowed to live his life forbade excesses of the type he intended. In 1567 he was about to leave the order in search of a stricter rule when he met Teresa of Ávila (see page

100), a fellow Carmelite who was attempting to establish religious houses in which the strict, original rule of the order of Our Lady of Mount Carmel would be followed. He became an enthusiastic recruit.

For almost a decade John of the Cross lived the lonely life of the ascetic in a small, reformed Carmelite community, which existed in extreme poverty in one of the remotest parts of central Spain. He ate barely enough to prevent himself from starving to death, he occupied a tiny, leaky hovel in which he could neither stand up nor lie down at full length, and he braved the extremes of heat and cold that the seasons brought in the middle of the Castilian plateau. He explained his reasons for doing this in his writings, which were subsequently published.

1 The soul that desires God to surrender Himself to it wholly must surrender to Him wholly and leave nothing for itself . . .
The affection and attachment which the soul has for creatures [*the technical word for material things*] renders the soul like to these
5 creatures; and the greater is its affection, the closer is the equality and likeness between them . . .
All the beauty of the creatures compared with the infinite beauty of God, is the height of deformity . . .
The light of divine union cannot dwell in the soul if these
10 affections [*for the creatures*] first flee not away from it.

His reputation attracted many recruits to the Discalced Carmelites (the reformed branch of the order, so called because its members gave up wearing shoes and wore sandals or went barefoot instead). This made him extremely unpopular with the Calced Carmelite majority. In 1577 they kidnapped him and held him a prisoner for eight months. In an effort to persuade him to abandon his practices, they alternately tortured him and attempted to bribe him with promises of promotion within the order. But they were unsuccessful. John regarded this treatment as merely another attempt by God to test his resolve. He used his time of suffering to write poetry explaining his beliefs and practices. After his escape from captivity he continued this literary work, over a period of time producing, among other things, a small collection of poems of the highest quality. He is regarded by many critics as having been Spain's most talented poet. He is also generally thought of as the person who provided the clearest insight into the Catholic branch of mysticism. His lasting reputation rests on these twin achievements.

Naturally, there are problems for the English-speaking student in appreciating this greatness. His poetry loses much in translation, and its meanings are obscure to those who do not appreciate the subtleties of mysticism. His intended audience was primarily fellow Catholics who had travelled far down the road of contemplation, and, although some of his thoughts were addressed to relative beginners, his writings remain largely inaccessible to the general reader. But, at least, it is possible to begin to appreciate the flavour of his work in stanzas addressed to God, such as:

1 Come, grant me thy fruition full and free!
  And henceforth do thou send
  No messenger to me,
  For none but thou my comforter can be.

John of the Cross finally found the contentment he sought, and in the process he exercised considerable influence over like-minded Catholics throughout the world. His example was a direct encouragement to the many who attempted to follow a similar path to spiritual perfection, and his writings quickly became standard works for those who wished to explore a route to religion through contemplation. But, of course, as a thinker rather than a doer, he represented no more than a minority fringe of the Catholic Reformation. His impact was limited by the fact that many of his sympathisers fell foul of the Inquisition, which mistrusted his apparent rejection of the 'props' of organised religion, while his teachings made sense only to those of an extreme persuasion. Yet John of the Cross was significant. He was a symbol of the spiritual re-awakening that took place within the Church during the Catholic Reformation. This was a phenomenon that owed nothing to the rise of Protestantism, and it would have occurred even had Luther never lived. It was part of a positive and independent resurgence of interest in spiritual matters. It was in no sense part of a defensive reaction. However, his impact was less than that of another Carmelite with whom his name is closely linked – Teresa of Ávila. Both were canonised and became saints of the Catholic Church.

2 Teresa of Ávila (1515–82)

John of the Cross had one great natural advantage over his more famous contemporary. He was a man. Teresa of Ávila was 'merely a woman'. This was a vital distinction in sixteenth-century Spain where sex stereotyping was extreme. Men were expected to be active and dominant. They lived public lives, being free to travel at will and to associate with whom they pleased. Women were expected to be passive and subservient, living their lives almost totally within the confines of their homes. A young girl had two possible futures ahead of her. She could either be married, normally in her early teens and often to a much older man, and face the prospect of annual pregnancies until her body was worn out. Or she could become a nun. Thousands of girls each year, especially from the ranks of the numerous families of the nobility, chose the latter course. Some acted from a sense of genuine vocation. They had been won over by the arguments in favour of abandoning the wicked world in order to seek God in the tranquillity of a convent.

Most, however, based their choice on more practical considerations. Fear of sex, and especially of childbirth, was widespread among girls and young women, many of whom had witnessed the sufferings of their mothers and had decided to avoid a similar fate for themselves. In any case, it was well understood that there were insufficient men available to provide all girls with husbands. The fact that many men had two or three wives in succession – for young married women commonly died in childbirth – did not make up for the loss of potential husbands through emigration to America or death on the battlefields of Europe. Women often entered a convent when it became clear that they were not going to attract a husband.

Teresa de Ahumada could, as a teenager, have had the pick of the men in the Castilian city of Ávila. Not only was she thought to be beautiful, both in looks and personality, but she also came from a well-connected and well-to-do family. Her father was likely to provide her with a large dowry and she seemed to be strong enough to produce many healthy children. But she was determined not to marry. As a young girl she had become frighteningly aware of how short life on earth was in comparison with eternity, and she had become very fearful of the possibility of eternal damnation.

1 All things are nothing, the world is vanity, life is short: I began to
 be afraid that if I died I should go to hell, and although I was not
 yet prepared to become a nun, I saw that it was the best and safest
 state of life: and so gradually I determined to force myself to enter
5 religion.

Although her father needed her to organise his household – her mother having died while giving birth to her youngest sister – she ran away to a convent when she was 20. She chose the Carmelite convent in Ávila because she had heard that conditions there were very comfortable. Her father, who was a very religious man, finally agreed to allow her to remain in the convent, to which her dowry was then paid. As a result of this generosity Teresa was allowed a private cell (in effect a self-contained flat), and could expect to be deferred to by the nuns from less exalted social backgrounds. The social life of the convent was extensive. Nuns were allowed to visit one another's cells, visitors could be entertained in the convent parlour, and extended periods could be spent away from the convent staying with friends and relations.

For more than 20 years Teresa enjoyed this undemanding existence. However, she was by no means totally worldly. She survived a number of spiritual crises, in which self-loathing and the resulting depression seriously endangered her life. As she recovered she found her consolation in 'contemplative prayer'. This was the main technique used by the mystics to rid themselves of earthly desires and to draw closer to God. By 1559 she had gained a reputation for saintliness throughout the city on account of her visions, ecstasies and raptures. In her visions she claimed not only to see Jesus but to have conversations with him. Her ecstasies and raptures appeared to outsiders as fainting fits or periods of unconsciousness during which her smiling face showed that she was experiencing pleasure rather than pain. Sometimes she was said to levitate. Teresa explained such happenings as visitations by the Holy Spirit which left her soul refreshed.

Visions and visitations were not unusual among Spanish nuns at the time. But they were very suspect among the all-male Church hierarchy, where they were generally considered to be either fraudulent, or the result of over-active female imaginations, or the work of the Devil. Some of Teresa's most famous contemporary visionaries had admitted under pressure that their experiences were no more than self-induced pretence, designed to gain them prestige among their peers. Those that could not be explained away in this manner were generally categorised as being the work of the Devil. As a matter of course, Teresa was forced to submit herself to detailed investigation by a sequence of reputable churchmen. Despite the fact that all of them pronounced her 'graces' to be the work of God and not of the Devil, she remained suspect in many people's eyes.

Nevertheless, Teresa continued to devote much of her time to her spiritual journey, following the well-trodden path of the mystics. She attempted to free herself from human desires by self-denial and long hours of quiet contemplation and prayer. She charted the course of her spiritual development in her writings, which when published after her death became popular treatises on the subject of prayer. In 1571 she achieved her ultimate ambition, described by her as her spiritual marriage with Jesus, whom she henceforth referred to as the bridegroom. She believed that he was now always with her, and she with him, and that he was constantly available to her to give her commands through prayer. The genuineness of her claim was widely believed at the time, and has been a source of inspiration for Catholics ever since. There is no doubt that she believed in the reality of her experiences.

* Yet it was not Teresa's graces that made her a significant figure of the Catholic Reformation. She is best remembered by historians as the foundress of a number of reformed (or Discalced) Carmelite convents and monasteries. By 1560 she had become greatly dissatisfied with the laxity of her current convent in which the nuns lived according to the 'mitigated' Carmelite rule, established by papal decree in the late fifteenth century. The mitigated rule had been introduced to all Carmelite houses because the primitive (original) rule, dating from the early Middle Ages, had been considered too harsh to suit the relaxed attitudes of the Renaissance period. Teresa had come to the conclusion that the relaxations allowed by the mitigated rule made it virtually impossible for nuns to concentrate on their primary duties of praising

God and preparing their souls for heaven. Her views were based on 25 years of first hand experience during which she, like her sister nuns, had frequently succumbed to the temptation to take an over-enthusiastic interest in worldly affairs. They had all spent hours engaged in idle chatter, both in their own cells and in the convent parlour where visitors had been frequently and eagerly entertained. They had become far too concerned with their appearance, devoting considerable time and effort to making their habits (clothes) as fashionable as possible, including the extensive use of jewellery. They had also taken trouble to ensure that their bodily comforts were well provided for. Fine cloth had been used to make their habits, their cells had been equipped with good quality bedding and furniture and the best available food had been purchased for their enjoyment.

Teresa was sure that nuns would lead more purposeful lives if they concentrated more of their attention on the worship of God. In the new convents she intended to found she wished to ensure that the nuns would be free from distractions. This was partly to be achieved by reducing the opportunities for conversation. Visiting each other within the convent was to be banned and visitors to the parlour were to be discouraged. In addition, enclosure was to be complete. Nuns were not to be allowed to leave the convent, and the spoken word was to be the only contact they were to have with their infrequent visitors. Not only were the nuns to wear black veils covering the whole of their faces, but they were to be hidden from the view of strangers behind grilles that allowed the passage of sound but nothing else. Teresa also thought that size was a major contributory factor to laxity. She saw little possibility of a large community, such as her present convent with 130 nuns, ever being able to be godly. She, therefore, set an upper limit of 13 nuns (later increased to 21) for her new convents. She also laid great stress on the careful selection of those who were to be admitted, as she was certain that quality as well as quantity was a problem in existing convents. This sometimes led her into difficulties with her benefactresses:

1 If Your Ladyship commands me, there's nothing more to be said, I shall obey. But I do ask Your Ladyship to reflect seriously and to want nothing but the best for your house. Where the nuns are few in number, the quality must be proportionately higher. On
5 my own account I shall not accept either of the two of whom you speak to me. I find in them neither sanctity, courage nor talents sufficient to be an advantage for the house.

Teresa also believed that greater physical hardship would help the nuns to concentrate their minds on God. She insisted that their clothing and bedding was to be of the coarsest material, that they were to fast frequently, that they were never to eat meat, and that they were to spin to earn the money for their food. But she was by no means an extremist on questions of self-denial. She was adamant that the regulations should be relaxed where their enforcement was genuinely likely to lead to health being damaged. She even went to considerable lengths to persuade those who were being excessively zealous to modify their behaviour. One of her particular dislikes was the over-use of discipline (the beating of oneself or each other as punishment for sins and in memory of the sufferings of Jesus on his way to Calvary to be crucified). In fact, she saw little merit and considerable danger in all extremes of self-imposed ill-treatment. She described herself attempting to convince John of the Cross and his followers of this:

1 I begged them not to give themselves up to penance with so much
   rigour . . . I was afraid the Devil might take this means to make
   an end of them before what I hoped for from these Fathers had
   been effected . . . [the Devil] sees the harm they can do him as
5 long as they are alive and leads them into the temptation of giving
   themselves up to crazy penances to destroy their health.

Teresa possessed great powers of persuasion when dealing with people face to face. In 1562 she finally succeeded in convincing the Bishop of Ávila to allow her to open a reformed convent in the city, despite widespread local opposition. For the next five years she lived quietly in her new foundation. Then she was visited by the Italian General of the Carmelite order who was keen to encourage the foundation of reformed houses. He issued her with letters patent allowing her to establish reformed convents (and up to two monasteries) throughout Castile, each of which would be under the control of the local bishop rather than of the Provincial, the local head of the order.

Between 1567 and 1581 Teresa opened a further 21 reformed houses. In each case there was a considerable struggle to win the necessary support. Extreme perseverance, often involving personal pleadings over several months, was normally required to obtain permission from each bishop, even when a rich benefactress had been found to contribute the funds for the establishment of the house. But the greatest opposition came from the existing Carmelite organisation in Spain. The venom of the Calced Carmelite opposition to Teresa was extreme. This reached its height in 1577 and 1578 with a co-ordinated campaign of personal vilification, physical harassment and political campaigning. Teresa was denounced to the Pope as a fraud who lived a life of sexual laxity (she was then in her early sixties), her manuscript autobiography was obtained by deception and was referred to the Inquisition as being heretical, some of her leading supporters (including John of the Cross) were abducted and illegally imprisoned and, by a mixture of implied threats and misinformation, important political figures were persuaded not to offer her support. However, by 1581 changes of personnel in key positions had resulted in those sympathetic to Teresa being once more in command. The Inquisition declared that Teresa had no case to answer, and the Pope not only accepted her detailed proposals for the rule to be followed in the discalced houses, but also agreed to the Calced and the Discalced Carmelites being independent of one another, each with their own structure of authority. Thus in her last months, Teresa received the comfort of the certain knowledge that the future of her foundations was secure.

3 Philip Neri (1515–95)

If Teresa was essentially a conformist, her Italian contemporary, Philip Neri, was a genuine 'breaker of the mould'. He was the most famous of the 'characters' of the Catholic Reformation. He was extremely unconventional. He went out of his way to shock all those he regarded as being 'stuffy', and he refused to allow anybody to hide from him behind social conventions. He wore his hat and sat down in the Pope's presence (thought to show a scandalous lack of respect), and he spoke to the mighty with mock civility, even putting his arm round them as he did so (generally interpreted as insolence). He acted the clown during formal ceremonies, and refused to play his part in ensuring solemnity at important occasions. He dressed in outrageous combinations of clothes, and appeared at one public celebration with one side of his face clean shaven and the other with a week's growth of beard. It was impossible either to intimidate or to influence him. People had either to accept him on his terms or have nothing to do with him.

Philip was born into a poor family in Florence. He drifted to Rome in his late teens, having received only a very rudimentary education. He soon became intensely religious (the cause is not known), and developed into a celebrity among the city's Florentine community because of his magnetic personality. In the 1540s he devoted much of this time to charitable work, especially with the incurably sick, and in 1551 he became a priest and took up a chaplaincy in his community's church. This launched him on the work for which he is best remembered – as the creator and leading light of the Roman Oratory.

The Roman Oratory began in a very small way as a daily meeting of eight male followers who listened to Philip reading from popular religious works and then discussed what they had heard. Everyone was free to express his own opinion. Frequent outings were also arranged. These were normally day-long rambles to visit the seven most sacred churches in Rome, with preaching, singing and praying along the way, and they attracted large attendances. As the popularity of the Oratory grew, and as more priests became involved on a regular basis, its activities became more formal and a distinction appeared between the priestly 'performers' and the lay 'spectators'. The readings turned into sermons and the discussion into a series of short presentations by younger priests. In 1575 the Pope formally recognised the 'Congregation of the Oratory', granting it the use of a run-down church and an unoccupied convent. Philip disliked the move towards organisation. While he lived the Oratory remained an *ad hoc* gathering of priests who provided for themselves, wore no uniform, and were free to join and leave the Congregation as they wished. The Congregation's Constitutions (formal rules) did not receive papal approval until 1612. By that time other Oratories, based on Philip Neri's model, but independent of the Roman brotherhood, had been founded in many Italian and French cities.

* Historians have tended to concentrate on Philip Neri's role as the founder of one of the Catholic Reformation's more interesting new organisations. But this is almost to parody the man, for he disliked formality of any kind. He saw himself as 'a free spirit' and he encouraged others to do 'their own thing'. He might have fitted in well with the flower people of the 1960s. He refused to be a conventional leader, and he would only infrequently tell others what to do. When he did issue instructions, they were rarely conventional. On more than one occasion he dragged a follower out of church and sent him to work in

St Philip Neri

the hospital, claiming that he had been praying for too long and that the time had come to serve God in other ways. He was only prepared for his followers to make rules for themselves as long as it was clearly understood that he would not obey them. He stoutly maintained that logic was the work of the Devil and refused to be persuaded by practicalities. He hated the conventions of fame. At best he contradicted, and at worst he hit, those who called him a saint. He refused to be made a cardinal and he treated his two followers who accepted the invitation as if they were dead.

What, then, prevented him from being treated as a 'nut case'? He was saved by his charisma. Nearly all those with whom he came into contact – including several Popes and many cardinals – fell under his spell. He was larger than life in all respects. He filled all the space wherever he was. One reluctant, wealthy follower described what happened to him:

1 He won me over so magnificently that I was never able to give him up. He used to accompany me in my carriage to get me to persevere in my religion, or else he would force me to follow him – a thing I have never done for anyone else – with many embraces
5 and other signs of affection. He was such a lovable person and had such a charming way with him that he could get anyone to do exactly what he wanted.

Most of his time in the second half of his life was spent in hearing confessions and acting as 'director of conscience' to a wide variety of people, both ordinary and famous. His watchword was joy. He accepted conventional morality, but he encouraged his followers to enjoy themselves as much as possible. He was hostile to over-strict discipline, whether self- or externally imposed, and no more expected to be obeyed than he intended to obey his betters as a matter of course. He believed that it was for each individual to follow the dictates of his own conscience, and not to abdicate the responsibility to others.

Despite Philip's dislike of being thought of as special, he was widely regarded as being a saint during his lifetime. He was, in fact, canonised in 1622. Part of the case for his sanctity was that he saw many visions and experienced many ecstasies. Some people claimed to have seen him levitate while saying mass (thought to be a sign of God's special favour), and his closest helpers reported that he frequently fell into long trances while carrying out his private devotions. Philip did all he could to discourage these happenings, which he suspected were not inspired by God. It is often claimed that much of his clowning was to change the atmosphere when he felt that he was moving towards a painful spiritual experience. He would even do this in the middle of a church service if necessary. But much of the respect he enjoyed in Rome had been earned by years of complete selflessness. He was constantly available to those who wanted his spiritual comfort – even after he had retired to bed – and he always took seriously whatever problem was brought to him. Although he frequently encouraged others to seek innocent pleasure, his own joy seemed to come only from helping others.

Yet in many ways he did not conform to the standard expectations of saintliness. He was certainly not perfect. He could be intolerant and hurtful. He was open in his dislike of women, whom he regarded as 'silly'; he judged people by their physical appearance, dismissing those he regarded as being ugly; he was impatient with those who were slow to understand his meaning, sometimes shouting the sentence that was presenting difficulties into their ears at short range; and many of his practical jokes, while causing amusement among the observers, were deeply embarrassing to those directly involved – one of his regular ploys was to call upon one of his young followers in public to carry out an action that he knew was impossible for him. In many ways he was not a nice man.

* However, Philip Neri was of significance within the Catholic Reformation. He represented a branch of Catholicism that was deeply spiritual but which carried its burden joyously and independently. Much of the sixteenth-century revival was characterised by intolerant puritanism and rigid discipline. While Popes were sweeping Rome clean of homosexuals, Philip was openly taking great pleasure from a non-physical relationship with the young boys who made up a significant part of his following. At the same time as the Jesuits were demanding complete obedience and military discipline from their members, Philip was refusing even to specify the penances for those who made their confession to him, arguing that they must decide for themselves what was appropriate. Although Philip's brand of Catholicism was only briefly within the mainstream of the movement, it illustrated the broad front on which the Catholic Reformation advanced. In future centuries his memory could always be recalled to deflate those who risked taking themselves too seriously.

4 Vincent de Paul (c1580–1660)

It is often claimed that the spiritual climax of the Catholic Reformation was reached in France during the reigns of Louis XIII (1610–43) and Louis XIV (1643–1715). This climax is partly perceived in terms of quality, but mainly it is a matter of quantity. The amount of spiritually-motivated activity that took place was indeed remarkable, and, because so much of it was inspired or at least supported by members of the ruling classes, it was particularly well documented. This, of course, has made it readily accessible to historians and the topic has been extensively researched.

The Catholic Reformation in France was urgently needed. In 1600 the Gallican Church (the Catholic Church in France) was at a very low ebb. It is possible that more than half of the religiously-minded population, (although only ten per cent of the total population), had been lured away from old allegiances by the powerful attraction of Calvinism, which had faced little competition from an essentially moribund Catholic Church. The reforms decreed by the Council of Trent had been almost totally ignored in France, and most of the abuses that had been long complained of remained uncorrected. In essence the Church organisation was made up of two completely separate groups of people. The senior hierarchy of archbishops, bishops, abbots, abbesses, cathedral canons and other diocesan office-holders was virtually exclusively recruited from among the younger children of aristocratic families, and the majority of them regarded their posts as sinecures, providing a source of income without the need to undertake any significant work. At the other extreme were the tens of thousands of parish priests, nearly all of whom were drawn from peasant families, and were only differentiated from their brothers by the fact that they drew a modest income in return for officiating (often incorrectly) at services in the local church. Many of them were largely uneducated, and used their considerable amounts of 'free' time to earn deserved reputations as drunkards and womanisers. It was a common saying in the south of France that the surest way of getting to hell was to become a priest.

In the early years of the seventeenth century a large number (hundreds rather than thousands) of wealthy French Catholics felt the need to do something about this situation. Their main motivation was a genuine concern for the spiritual well-being of the majority of the population who were not receiving the religious 'nurture' they required. They were inspired by a small number of outstanding clerics who had the ability to transform good intentions into positive action, several of whom were subsequently canonised by the Pope. The most famous of these saints was Vincent de Paul, known in France as 'Monsieur Vincent'.

* A great deal is known about Vincent de Paul. His opinions and beliefs on a wide range of issues are extensively documented in the thousands of surviving letters of advice and guidance that he wrote to his followers. Yet, there is uncertainty over some of the basic facts of his life. He was born into a poor peasant family in Gascony, and no record of his date of birth was kept. His biographers have made various informed guesses about this, and various dates have found their way into general histories of the period, often in the guise of established facts. However, none of these can be relied on. It is, for example, frequently asserted that he was born in 1576. But this date was merely the guess of his first biographer based on the known fact that he was ordained in 1600, at which time he should, according to canon law, have been at least 24. However, it appears that he was almost certainly ordained under age, as the best available evidence (Vincent's own

statements about his age, made in the 1630s) strongly suggests that he was born in either 1580 or 1581.

Vincent de Paul was not a very admirable young man. He was a highly intelligent child, who was rescued from rural obscurity as an act of charity by a magistrate from the local town, who paid for his education. Entry to the priesthood was a natural progression from such a beginning. The Church provided the most obvious escape route from poverty for the talented children of the lower strata of society. Vincent was an outstanding example of this process. His lack of social connections naturally meant that he was unable to secure appointment to any well-paid position. However, his powerful personality and outstanding intelligence, allied to a shrewd awareness of how to 'work the system', made him an acceptable person for pious members of the aristocracy to employ as a junior member of their household. Throughout his twenties he appears to have been a typical self-seeking cleric of ability, ingratiating himself with the rich and powerful in the hope of future preferment. It is not known what happened to transform him into the man of transparent goodness, who gave no thought to his own welfare, that he became during his thirties. It is tempting to conclude that he came to believe in the act he put on for his wealthy benefactors, and that he decided to devote the same drive and energy to goodness that he had previously devoted to ambition.

* Whatever the cause, the effects were very apparent. He possessed the ability to make people feel pleased at doing good. He used this to extract large sums of money from the rich in order to support the ventures that his creative imagination and his extensive organisational skills had originated. His earliest, longest-lasting and most effective initiative was in recruiting women for charitable works. In 1617 he founded the Ladies of Charity, an organisation which arranged for well-to-do women to spend some of their spare time visiting the old, the sick, and the poor. Within a decade there were over 100 groups of ladies within the organisation. However, Vincent was dissatisfied with the impact of his first foundation. Much of the assistance required by the underprivileged depended on someone being prepared to undertake menial tasks on a regular and time-consuming basis. This the ladies were unwilling to do.

In 1633, therefore, Monsieur Vincent accepted the argument that what was required was an organisation that could be joined on a full-time basis by any woman, irrespective of her social standing. He founded the Daughters of Charity (known as the Gray Sisters because of the colour of their uniforms) as an open order, living communally, but not bound by the vows taken by nuns. Throughout Vincent's lifetime an average of two new houses of the order were founded every year, and the growth has continued ever since, spreading throughout the Catholic world. Much of the work of the Gray Sisters has been in nursing the sick in hospitals, but they have been used to minister to the needy wherever they are to be found – in prisons, on the streets, on the battlefield and in their own homes. The cumulative effect of the Sisters' social work has been enormous over the centuries, yet during the early years of their existence their major significance was as a precedent. The Church had traditionally been very suspicious of organisations for women that were neither enclosed nor regulated by traditional vows. The recognition of the Daughters of Charity was a real breakthrough. It paved the way for the foundation of dozens of similar orders in succeeding centuries.

* However, it would be misleading to give the impression, as many general histories have done, that Vincent de Paul's primary concern was with caring for the physical needs of the underprivileged. His main interest was undoubtedly the spiritual welfare of his fellow human beings. The second of his major foundations was the Mission of France (1625). The aim of the Mission was to bring effective preaching and the proper administering of the sacraments to the French countryside, where the benefits of religion were largely absent. Each of the Mission's ventures lasted for several months and was staffed by a group of specially trained priests who, in the words of the foundation document, had undertaken

1 to renounce their city life . . . in order to apply themselves entirely and purely to the salvation of poor people, going from village to village at the expense of their common purse, to preach, instruct, exhort and teach catechism to those poor folk . . .
5 [They] should not leave a village until everybody has been instructed in the things necessary for salvation, and until each person has made a confession.

By 1660 there were 131 priests with 52 lay helpers in the Mission, organised into 23 houses. 840 missions had taken place, mostly in rural areas, but also in a few of the notoriously godless urban centres. The approach throughout had been to win converts by the simplicity of the message and the humility of its bearers. Vincent's constant reminder to his missionaries was that

1 We do not believe a man because he is learned, but because we esteem and love him.

The winning of this esteem and love meant that the missionaries had to live within a community for long enough to become accepted. This willingness to devote time to a community was the secret of the Mission's considerable success. Although no reliable statistics exist to substantiate the verdict of historians that the Mission was responsible for much of the religious re-awakening within the seventeenth-century Gallican Church, there is ample anecdotal evidence to suggest that tens of thousands of Frenchmen, both nominal Catholics and Huguenots, acquired a genuine commitment to the Church as a result of the Mission's endeavours.

* Vincent de Paul, in common with most committed churchmen of the time, was also deeply concerned about the generally poor quality of the priesthood in France. Not only were most of them uneducated and untrained, but they were also lacking in faith. Many of them were completely unfitted to carry out their duties. But Vincent was in no position to tackle the problem in a coherent manner. He could only attempt to improve the situation in a piecemeal fashion. From 1628 onwards he organised a series of 'Retreats for Ordinands', whereby those about to become priests received a 20-day 'crash course' on the duties of their calling. It was little enough, but it was significantly better than nothing. Within a few years attendance at a retreat had become an essential prerequisite for ordination in about a third of French dioceses. In the years after 1643 there was a rapid increase in the number of seminaries (training colleges for priests) in France. The Lazarists – as members of the Mission were popularly called after the headquarters in Paris – were at the forefront of this development, and they had opened seven seminaries before Vincent died. Although the courses run at the Lazarist seminaries were short – varying from six months to two years – and concentrated solely on training and faith-building rather than on wider educational objectives, the 400 priests who were trained each year were infinitely better equipped than most of their forerunners currently in service.

Vincent did not entirely ignore the needs of existing priests. He initiated a sequence of one-day in-service training courses, known as Tuesday Conferences, and his example was widely and lastingly followed throughout much of the country. As a result, it quickly became accepted as the norm that serving priests would spend one day each week in retreat with their colleagues, increasing their knowledge and skills and deepening or renewing their faith. Although it is impossible to quantify the effect of this development, it is widely believed that it made a significant contribution to the spiritual elevation of Catholicism in France. Vincent de Paul deserves credit as its effective initiator, despite the fact that most of the work was done by others.

* Catholic commentators have tended to be uncritical in their assessment of Vincent de Paul's contribution to the spiritual awakening of the Church in France. They have often portrayed him as the totally virtuous implementer of God's will. This is certainly how Vincent saw himself from about 1620 onwards. He regarded himself as a true mystic, who had disciplined his own desires so that they had no effect on his actions. He exhorted his followers to be similarly open to receiving instructions from God:

1 Take care not to spoil God's works by trying to hurry them too

much. Take good time and know how to wait. Too often we spoil
good works by going too fast, because we are acting according to
our own inclinations. What the good God wishes done is accom-
5 plished almost by itself, without our thinking of it. Do the good
that presents itself to be done. I do not say we should go out
indiscriminately and take on everything, but rather those things
He wants of us. We belong to Him and not to ourselves.

It seems that part of Vincent's effectiveness was the result of his
willingness to please his large number of powerful benefactors, including the Queen, by treating their suggestions for action as inspired by
God. This, perhaps the ultimate in unintended flattery, meant that he
was always welcomed in ruling circles. It also presented him with
opportunities to influence policy at the highest levels, especially over
matters such as the appointment of bishops. Although he was not able
to reverse the practice of selecting new bishops from among the
country's ruling families, he was able to establish the principle that
those appointed should be both formally educated and well disposed to
carry out the duties of the post. However, his openness to suggestions
from the social élite did have one obvious consequence. There was little
pattern to the enormous range of developments he initiated, and there
was a tendency for nothing to be carried through to a conclusion.
Fortunately for the well-being of his ventures, he was able to attract a
large number of energetic 'finishers' to serve beside him. Thus much of
what he started eventually bore fruit.

Making notes on 'The Spirit of the Catholic Reformation'

You are unlikely ever to need to write in detail about any of the four
saints featured in this chapter. But you are likely to need to use them as
examples in a discussion on the nature of the Catholic Reformation. So
your notes should concentrate on identifying the ways in which each of
the four typified some aspect of the revival of spirituality within the
Church. However, you do not need to remember the details of the lives
of John of the Cross, Teresa of Ávila, Philip Neri, or Vincent de Paul,
so there is little point in noting them.
    It will probably be most convenient to make your notes under the
four section headings used in the chapter. For each person attempt to
answer the questions, 'What was the nature of his/her spirituality?' and
'What was his/her significance in the history of the Catholic Church?'
Include evidence to support each aspect of your answers. Do not think
about each character in isolation. Attempt to identify similarities and
differences between them.

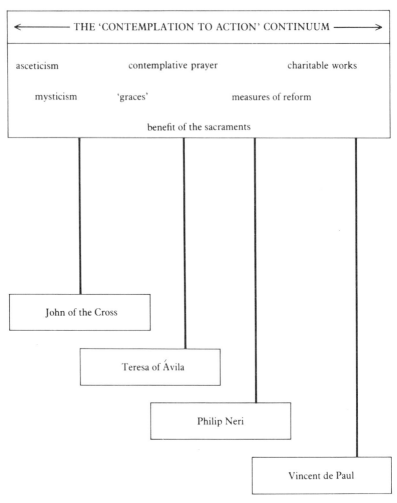

Summary – The Spirit of the Catholic Reformation

Source-based questions on 'The Spirit of the Catholic Reformation'

1 John of the Cross and Mysticism
Read the extracts from John of the Cross's writings on pages 99 and 100. Answer the following questions:

a) What reasons does John of the Cross give in the first extract for wanting to lose his love of 'creatures'?

b) What aim of mysticism is stated in the second extract?

c) What did John of the Cross do in an effort to lose his love of 'creatures'? Answer this question from the knowledge you have gained from reading this chapter.

2 Teresa of Ávila

Read the extracts from Saint Teresa's writings on pages 101, 103 and 104. Answer the following questions:

a) In the first extract, what does Teresa say motivated her to become a nun?

b) What characteristics does Teresa display in the second and third extracts?

c) Identify which two of the extracts are from Teresa's autobiography, and which one is from her collected letters. Give reasons for your answers.

d) What is the significance of the use of the Devil in the reasoning used in the third extract?

3 The appeal of Philip Neri

Read the description of Philip Neri's appeal on page 107 and study his portrait reproduced on page 106. Answer the following questions:

a) Using only the evidence contained in the extract, describe the techniques used by Philip Neri to win the support of the author.

b) What evidence in the extract suggests that the author was a reluctant convert?

c) What is the author's opinion of Philip Neri? Explain your answer in detail.

d) The portrait was painted in 1647 and was intended to be displayed in the church that the Pope had assigned to the Roman Oratory. What was the artist attempting to communicate in his portrait? Explain your answer in detail.

e) Compare and contrast these two pieces of evidence about Philip Neri.

4 Vincent de Paul and the Mission

Read the extracts given on pages 111 and 112–13. Answer the following questions:

a) What is the implication of the phrase 'to renounce their city life' in the first line of the first extract?

b) What evidence do the extracts provide about the methods employed by the Mission?

c) How far does the second extract provide an explanation of the somewhat random nature of Vincent de Paul's achievements?

CHAPTER 7

The International Politics of the Catholic and Counter Reformations

Most modern-day students have grown up with a clear awareness of the concepts of both a divided community (by race, by religion, by wealth, by age) and of a divided world (developed and developing, rich and poor, east and west). The common patterns of thought resulting from an acceptance of the idea of such divisions – especially the widespread use of the collective 'them' and the collective 'us' – have for long been apparent in the tendency to seek answers to problems by confrontation rather than by working for consensus and co-operation. Unthinking support of one's own group – be it a racial, religious or national grouping, or even the supporters of a football club – together with hostility towards those who are different, is the norm in most modern societies. This has been the case in Europe for many centuries. From about 1550 to about 1650 the antagonism between Catholics and Protestants was the most striking example of this. At times, the mutual antagonism was so virulent that many contemporaries viewed western Europe as being divided into two armed camps which were ranged against each other. Until a generation ago most historians took this contemporary perception at face value.

Yet despite the significance of the division between the two major organised branches of European Christianity, it was rarely the determining factor in international politics. More normally, it was a backcloth against which the actors played their parts. This is not to suggest that religious issues did not really matter, but rather that most statesmen were prepared to sacrifice the interests of religion if this was demanded by the selfish needs of the moment. It was not that international affairs were conducted solely by cynical hypocrites, merely that the interests of religion were uppermost in few rulers' minds. In most situations the advancement of the cause of one's religious grouping was a genuine objective, but it was one among many, and one that often had to be compromised.

In addition, the propaganda of the time which attempted to portray a united Catholic bloc and a similarly homogenous Protestant bloc is very misleading. Neither group was coherent, and internal struggles were often as significant as those between the groups. Of course, this was a long-established norm within the Catholic world. Ever since the emergence of the Bishop of Rome as the spiritual leader of western Christendom in the early Middle Ages, there had existed the potential for major disputes between secular rulers and the Pope. These usually arose when either the Pope attempted to increase his influence in the internal affairs of a state, or a ruler tried to obtain greater control over the Church within his territories. Such struggles continued unabated throughout the era of the Catholic and Counter Reformations, especially as rulers sought to capitalise on the Pope's need for their support. Although no similar source of conflict existed within the Protestant camp, the variations in the organisation and teachings of different state churches were often sufficient to weaken commitment to a common purpose. This was particularly so with the Lutheran and Calvinist churches. They often treated their Protestant co-religionists as if *they* were the real enemy.

Historians with a traditional perception of the Counter Reformation as a struggle against Protestantism have stressed the significance of the efforts by Catholics to win back the territories that had been lost, especially in the Empire, the Netherlands and Britain. It is this emphasis, and its shortcomings, that is explored within this chapter.

1 Ferdinand and Isabella

In this context it is perhaps ironic that the most significant of the early exchanges in the international politics of the Catholic and Counter Reformations took place between the Pope and the monarchs of Spain. Ferdinand and Isabella jointly ruled Spain from 1479 to 1504 as a personal union of Aragon and Castile. Long before the birth of Protestantism they progressively extracted permission from a succession of Popes to exercise almost independent control over the Church within their territories. Most of the painstaking diplomatic activity that lay behind these changes was undertaken by King Ferdinand. But it was Queen Isabella (often known as Isabella the Catholic) who took advantage of the relative freedom from papal interference to implement a large scale reformation of the Spanish Church. In the fourth quarter of the fifteenth century, many of the changes took place in Spain that the Council of Trent was not to propose for introduction elsewhere until more than half a century later. This guaranteed that the country would remain the pace-setter within the Catholic world throughout the sixteenth century.

2 Charles V

The task of resisting the spread of Protestantism during its early decades fell to Charles V, Ferdinand and Isabella's grandson. He was the Holy Roman Emperor (1519–56), as well as the ruler of the Burgundian lands (which included the Netherlands) and of the Spanish kingdoms. As Holy Roman Emperor he inherited a responsibility for defending the interests of the Catholic Church. He took this responsibility very seriously. It would have been far easier for him if he had not, for his commitment to the Church limited his room for manoeuvre in the other passion of his life – the struggle for European supremacy with the Valois kings of France. It also left him vulnerable to the plotting of his less scrupulous enemies, who were prepared to take advantage of his dedication to the Church to ally with those to whom Charles was opposed on religious grounds. Thus the French were not only prepared to ally with the Lutheran states in Germany in order to apply pressure to Charles. They also used their influence to delay the convening of the general council that Charles hoped would reach a settlement with the Protestants (see page 43), and they were even prepared to join forces with the Muslims of the Ottoman Empire in an effort to distract Charles from his main purposes. This latter action scandalised much of European civilised society. The common expectation was that Christian rulers would stand shoulder to shoulder to resist the infidel.

The actions of the French were not the only complicating factor for Charles in dealing with what he came to think of as 'the Protestant menace'. If he had been the direct ruler of the territory in which Martin Luther began his revolt against the authority of the Pope, he would have been able to intervene decisively. But he was not. As Emperor he was the ruler 'at one remove'. Although his was the final political authority throughout the Empire, he was able to do little without the acquiescence of the princes and city councils who formed the first level of government. This agreement was increasingly difficult to obtain as more and more princes and city governments recognised the advantages of ending their religious allegiance to Rome. They saw that not only would large sums of money no longer need to cross the Alps to satisfy 'the greed of the Papacy', but that it would be possible for some of the Church's wealth to be diverted into their own coffers. There were also potential political advantages to be gained in the process of consolidating their power within their territories. The traditional system allowed final decisions on many vital local issues, especially those relating to matrimony and inheritance, to be made in Rome. A ruler who adopted Protestantism would be able to decide such matters at home where he could probably exercise decisive influence on the outcome. Thus there was little incentive for princes and city councils to resist the demands of vociferous minorities of their citizens to declare for Protestantism, even if it meant incurring the Emperor's anger.

During the 1520s and 1530s Charles was only prepared to give vent to his displeasure in words. He felt that he could not afford to alienate the rulers of the Protestant states in Germany. He hoped to win their active support, in the form of financial contributions towards the cost of his armies for the defence of his territories against France and the Ottoman Empire. At the very least, he aimed to maintain their neutrality. His strategy, therefore, was one of appeasement. He attempted to satisfy the Protestants by allowing them to continue undisturbed as long as they were prepared to search with him for a compromise agreement that would be acceptable to both Catholics and Protestants, and as long as they were willing to promise to do nothing to encourage further defections from Rome.

From the early 1540s Charles was less willing to be conciliatory. The immediate threats from France and the Turks had been removed, and the practicability of reaching an accommodation with the Protestants, leading to a re-unification of the Church, was in serious doubt following the failure of the talks at Regensburg in 1541. Charles now felt strong enough to crush the German Protestants by force of arms. He made careful diplomatic preparations. He disrupted the unity of the Protestant states by secretly luring the Duke of Saxony to his side with promises of land and honours. He also ensured that the Lutherans' erstwhile ally, France, remained neutral. In two seasons of campaigning in 1546 and 1547 the Protestant armies were destroyed. It now seemed that Charles was about to become the hero of the Counter Reformation. But it was not to be.

Charles was unable to translate his military victories into lasting political achievements. When he attempted to utilise the undisputed mastery of his armies to impose his will in the internal religious affairs of the Empire he was met by the resistance of Catholic and Protestant states alike. Both groups were prepared to lay aside their sectarian differences in order to present a united front against the threatened increase in Imperial political power. The Catholic rulers were prepared to accept the continued existence of Protestantism rather than to agree to political changes within the Empire that threatened to result in the princes becoming the virtual servants of a strong central government. Given that his armies were insufficiently large to occupy more than a tiny portion of the Empire at any one time, Charles had no realistic option but to agree with the princes that there should be no wholesale replacement of Lutheran rulers by Catholics. Force of arms had proved to be a delusion.

Charles slowly came to the realisation that he was not going to solve the Protestant problem in Germany. His attempts to conclude a compromise agreement by direct negotiations had failed; his destruction of the Protestants' capability for military resistance had achieved little; and events at the Council of Trent in 1552, when Protestant delegates arrived with impossible demands, confirmed that a general council was not going to be able to heal the breach. There was no other acceptable political way forward. In 1555 Charles, recognising that he could achieve nothing more, handed over power in Germany to his brother, Ferdinand, and retired to solitude in Spain. A year later he formally abdicated his thrones. His son Philip became King of Spain and ruler of the Burgundian lands. Ferdinand became Holy Roman Emperor.

Ferdinand moved quickly to settle the issue on the best terms available to him. The Peace of Augsburg (1555) recognised that Lutheranism, as a series of independent churches, would continue to exist. It was agreed that each ruler of the Empire would be free to chose

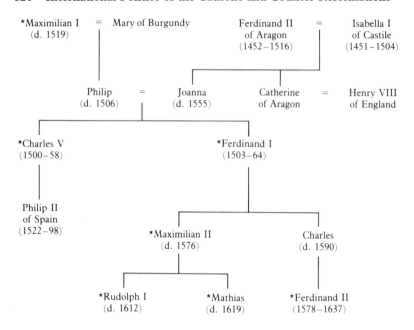

Holy Roman Emperors are indicated by *

The descent of the Habsburgs

between Catholicism and Lutheranism, and that the general population would be forced either to adopt the religion of their ruler or to move elsewhere. This was just the type of surrender, accepting the permanence of the schism, that Charles had been unwilling to contemplate.

* Historians have been interested to speculate on the reasons for Charles's lack of success in his dealings with the German Protestants. Certainly his failure was unexpected at the time. Few contemporaries could have imagined that a group of religious dissidents would be permanently able to flaunt the wishes of the most powerful ruler Europe had seen since Charlemagne, seven centuries earlier. This has led some commentators to question Charles's commitment to the re-establishment of the unity of the Church. Such reservations are understandable, because it is certainly possible to argue that Charles failed to make the destruction of Protestantism his highest priority soon enough. His actions seem to show that he regarded both the struggle with France and the defence of western Europe against further Ottoman incursions as of greater importance. It appears that his policy was to concentrate on one issue at a time, with the result that it took many years for Protestantism to come to the top of the list.

Yet in some ways this is misleading. The manner in which Charles dealt with Lutheranism in Germany was probably more the result of miscalculation than a reflection of low priority. It is perhaps understandable that someone who was facing challenges in all directions should first have dealt with matters that were both important and urgent rather than with other important issues that seemed less pressing. It is little wonder that the intention of the Turks to capture Vienna and to spill over into central Europe should have attracted most of Charles's attention in the late 1530s, and that the threat of attack from France should have engrossed him periodically throughout his reign. In comparison, the religious problems of Germany must have appeared much less demanding of his time, even if he considered them to be just as important. But, of course, Charles had made two mistakes. He had assumed that it would be possible to use reasoned arguments to solve the problems Luther posed, failing to recognise that the Protestants had committed themselves to uncompromising stances, especially in rejecting the authority of the Pope. He had also judged that it would be soon enough to concentrate on religious matters once he had achieved his dynastic aspirations. But, as events proved, this was not so. The spread of Lutheranism had gone too far to be reversed when at last the Emperor took decisive action in the mid-1540s.

However, it would be very unfair to claim that Charles's failure to achieve his goals in his dealings with the Lutherans was entirely his own fault. It is true that he made mistakes, but he was not helped by those who should have shared the responsibility for restoring Church unity with him. The Popes of the period undermined his attempts to secure a compromise solution by adamantly refusing to implement either the organisational or the doctrinal reforms that might have satisfied the more moderate Protestants. Their view was that the German heretics must admit the error of their ways and seek forgiveness for their transgressions, but there was no realistic possibility that this would happen. In addition, other Catholic rulers, especially the kings of France and the princes of the Empire, were more interested in extracting political advantage from the situation than in ending the schism. The re-unification of the Church was clearly a low priority for them.

3 Philip II

It was during the reign of Charles V's son, Philip II (1556–1598), as King of Spain and ruler of its empire in Italy and the Americas, and of the Burgundian lands, that the political Counter Reformation took its clearest form. This was partly because of Philip's beliefs and attitudes. He thought of himself as being commissioned by God to ensure as many converts as possible to 'His true Church'. He was a conscientious man who generally stuck to his principles, and thus was not easily shaken in his resolve, even when it was apparent that his religiously-inspired policies were not in his own best interests. Yet he did not see himself as being in any sense the 'tool' of the Papacy. He believed that his commission came directly from God and he did not welcome any interference from the Pope. His view was that if the Pope cared to support his policies this was an advantage. But he did not consider it to be a prerequisite.

Fortunately for the unity of the Catholic cause, Philip's aggressive, counter-attacking views largely coincided with those of the Popes of the period. This was most noticeably so with Pius V (1566–72). Both thought of England as being of vital importance, being the most powerful of the non-Catholic states. Over a period of more than a decade, it became clear that Elizabeth I (1558–1603), despite her conciliatory words and vague promises, was not going to return her country to the Catholic fold. She was prepared to tolerate Catholics in her lands as long as they remained in secret, but she was not prepared to accept any formal or informal links with Rome. This policy of 'live and let live' was attractive neither to Philip nor to Pius. They demanded that Elizabeth be either the Church's friend or its enemy. When she refused to declare herself its friend, they assumed that she was its enemy.

★ In 1570 Pius V issued the Bull *Regnans in Excelsis*. It stated:

1 3. . . . Resting upon the authority of Him whose pleasure it was to place us (though unequal to such a burden) upon this supreme justice-seat, we do out of the fullness of our apostolic power declare the foresaid Elizabeth to be a heretic and favourer of
5 heretics, and her adherence in the matters aforesaid to have incurred the sentence of excommunication and to be cut off from the unity of the body of Christ.

4. And moreover [we declare] her to be deprived of her pretended title to the aforesaid crown and of all lordship, dignity and
10 privilege whatsoever.

5. And also [declare] the nobles, subjects and people of the said realm, and all others who have in any way sworn oaths to her, to be forever absolved from such an oath and from any duty arising from lordship, fealty and obedience . . . We charge and com-
15 mand all and singular the nobles, subjects, peoples and others aforesaid that they do not dare obey her orders, mandates and laws. Those who shall act to the contrary we include in the like sentence of excommunication.

This was tantamount to a declaration of war, and was regarded as such by Elizabeth. As a result, Catholics in England rapidly came under suspicion of being enemies of the state, and powers were taken to deal with those who attempted to publicise the Bull. An Act of 1571 stated:

1 And yet nevertheless divers seditious and very evil disposed

people . . . minding, as it should seem, very seditiously and
unnaturally not only to bring this realm and the imperial crown
thereof (being in very deed of itself most free) into the thraldom
5 and subjection of that foreign, usurped, and unlawful jurisdiction, preeminence and authority claimed by the said see of Rome,
but also to estrange and alienate the minds and hearts of sundry
her Majesty's subjects from their dutiful obedience . . . have
lately procured and obtained to themselves from the said bishop
10 of Rome and his said see divers bulls and writings, the effect
whereof hath been and is to absolve and reconcile all those that
will be contented to forsake their due obedience to our most
gracious sovereign lady the Queen's Majesty, and to yield and
subject themselves to the said feigned, unlawful and usurped
15 authority . . .

The Act went on to lay down penalties for those convicted of circulating
the Bull:

1 That then all and every such act and acts, offence and offences,
shall be deemed and adjudged by the authority of this Act to be
high treason, and the offender and offenders therein, their
procurers, abettors and counsellors to the fact and committing of
5 the said offence or offences, shall be deemed and adjudged high
traitors to the Queen and the realm; and being thereof lawfully
indicted and attained, according to the course of the laws of this
realm, shall suffer pains of death, and also lose and forfeit all their
lands, tenements, hereditaments, goods and chattels.

The government's hostility was particularly strong in the case of
priests who had been trained abroad and who were smuggled back into
the country as missionaries in increasing numbers from 1577. Because
some of them were more interested in plotting rebellions than in serving
the spiritual needs of the many remaining English Catholics, they all
came to be branded as spies and traitors. In an Act of 1581, further
powers were taken against them:

1 . . . all persons whatsoever which shall by any ways or means put
into practice to absolve, persuade or withdraw any of the Queen's
Majesty's subjects from their natural obedience to her Majesty, or
to withdraw them for that intent from the religion now by her
5 Highness' authority established within her Highness' domains to
the Romish religion, or to move them to promise any obedience to
any pretended authority of the see of Rome, or of any other
prince, state or potentate . . . shall be to all intents adjudged to be
traitors, and being thereof lawfully convicted shall have judg-
10 ment, suffer and forfeit as in case of high treason.

These powers were made even more specific in 1585 when Jesuits and other foreign-trained priests were given 40 days to leave the country or risk the death penalty. Few, if any, took advantage of the chance to leave in peace, and large numbers (variously estimated between 123 and 187) of them were captured and executed, mostly in the 1580s. Yet the supply did not dry up. The seminary that had been established at Douai in the Netherlands in 1568 continued to pour forth priests, nearly all the sons of the English Catholic gentry, who were prepared to risk their lives by returning home. Over 400 of them are known to have crossed the Channel to England during Elizabeth's reign. They were joined by numbers of Jesuits who had been specifically trained in Rome for the English Mission. However, their success seems to have been very limited. Their plottings were all abortive – mainly because of their own incompetence rather than because of the watchfulness of the authorities – and there was no apparent increase in the number of English Catholics. This, of course, is hardly surprising. To declare openly for the Pope was not only unpatriotic at a time when English nationalism was strong, but it was also to risk a heavy fine or imprisonment. The government had responded to the attack on it by making it more difficult for English Catholics to retain their old beliefs in peace.

Philip was more than prepared to assist the process of overthrowing Elizabeth, although he was furious that Pius had not consulted with him before issuing his Bull. Some historians have suggested that Philip's policy was nothing more than political self-interest dressed up in a religious guise. This argument has much to recommend it. It is clear that Philip had a great deal to gain from the weakening of England by the removal of a very able and independent-minded monarch and her replacement by someone who would depend on Spanish support to remain in power. It would both extend the area of Spanish influence and remove a growing annoyance. English seamen were becoming a serious nuisance to Spain in the Americas and Elizabeth was known to be a secret supporter of her undisciplined subjects. A friendly government in London would almost certainly take action to control the pirates.

This interpretation is supported by the selective way in which Philip intervened outside his territories in the Catholic cause. Besides his attempts to implement the papal Bull *Regnans in Excelsis* against Elizabeth, his only other foreign venture against the Protestants was in France, where he somewhat belatedly offered assistance to the Catholic League during the Wars of Religion. It could be argued that he only intervened when it appeared that the Huguenots might prevail and perhaps restore France to her former position as a great power. His non-intervention until then might have been because he was more than satisfied to see his greatest rival tear herself apart in a series of inconclusive civil wars. It was noticeable that he gave no assistance to the Catholics of Germany, where he had nothing to gain from the outcome of events. Although the evidence is far from conclusive, it would seem to be reasonable to suggest that, at best, Philip always ensured that his religious zeal abroad was likely to result in some political advantage to Spain.

* The orthodox view used to be that the struggle between Philip and his rebellious subjects in the Netherlands was also an integral part of the Counter Reformation. The protracted warfare that resulted in the eventual independence of the United Provinces (Holland) was seen as a contest between the Catholic Philip and the Protestant Dutch. On the surface this was a quite reasonable interpretation given Philip's statements about his commitment to the Catholic Church, and the facts that the rebellion seemingly started as a result of Philip's attempt to force Catholic uniformity on his Burgundian inheritance, the rebel leaders were all, or quickly became, Protestants, Elizabeth actively supported the rebels with troops and money, and the United Provinces, once independent, was a resolutely Protestant state. However, careful research has long disproved this theory. It has been shown that religion was the motivating force for only a very small minority of the rebels, and that the majority of Protestants in the Netherlands lived in the portion of the country that remained under Spanish rule, while the majority of the Dutch were Catholics at the time of their *de facto* independence in 1609.

However, it would be unreasonable to dismiss the Dutch rebellion against Spanish rule as a significant part of the Counter Reformation merely because religion can be shown to have been of minor importance in the minds of most of the rebels. Perhaps it is a case where the public perception of reality was more important than the reality itself. In Holland, Germany and England the struggle was publicised, at the time and later, as one element of the wider struggle between Protestantism and Catholicism, and much of the support, moral and material, that the rebels received from abroad was forthcoming because of this perception. Without the diplomatic assistance that the Dutch received from the Protestant 'bloc', it is possible that they would have failed to establish their independence. The lengthy struggle in the Netherlands, spanning a period of more than 70 years, was clearly a major contributory factor to the establishment of the political Counter Reformation as a historical concept.

4 The Empire

It was in the Holy Roman Empire that many of the most dramatic political events of the Counter Reformation confrontation between Catholicism and Protestantism took place. During the early decades of the Reformation the Protestants had had things very much their own way, despite the efforts made by Charles V to halt their progress. Even the Peace of Augsburg (1555), which had been intended to safeguard the orthodoxy of the territories of the church states (states ruled over by bishops or archbishops) and the remaining Catholic lay rulers within the Empire, had not seriously interrupted the spread of Protestantism. Most of the remaining independent bishoprics of north-eastern Germany had passed into Protestant hands by 1600. In fact, such was the appeal of the new faith to a significant minority of the population in most of the states of Germany, that only the most savage of repressions could have halted the development of an expanding Protestant nucleus in each Catholic territory. This was particularly the case as many of the newly converted Protestants were members of the noble or landowning classes. They were in a better position to defend themselves from possible government attack than their social inferiors would have been. Their potential vulnerability was reduced by their rulers' lack of either ready instruments of repression, such as the Inquisition, or the power within their own territories to introduce these measures easily.

Given this situation, how was it that any political Counter Reformation at all took place in Germany? In part it happened because the championing of the Catholic cause coincided with the selfish interests of some princes. Absolutist forms of government were becoming increasingly 'popular' in ruling circles, and the enforcement of religious orthodoxy offered princes an opportunity to extend their powers at the expense of their leading subjects. It also presented them with the possibility of extending their power outside their borders by championing a moral and seemingly unselfish cause. But there were also some rulers with a deep-felt commitment to the defeat of Protestantism. Many of these came from two families – the Wittelsbachs and the Habsburgs.

The three successive members of the Wittelsbach family who ruled Bavaria as its dukes from 1550–1651 were consistent in their desire to cleanse their south German state of heresy. Maximilian I (1597–1651), in particular, was determined to take firm action to erode the position of his many powerful Protestant subjects, and was prepared finally to expel all those who would not declare themselves to be Catholics. Thus one secure base for the Counter Reformation within the Empire was established. It had been prepared for by the energetic manner in which earlier dukes had insisted that the decrees of the Council of Trent should be implemented, and by the work of the Jesuits in ensuring that much of each rising generation of leading Bavarians received a sound Catholic schooling. Maximilian I, himself, had been educated by them.

However, Maximilian's predecessors, Albert V (1550–79) and William V (1579–97), had not been content to champion the Catholic cause within their own territories. They had used the issue of religion as a vehicle for furthering their dynastic ambitions. In particular they had attempted to prevent further Church territories in southern or western Germany being lost to the Protestants. They were even prepared to use armed force where necessary, especially if such action resulted in family gain, as in 1585 when the Duke's younger son became Archbishop-Elector of Cologne, in addition to being the existing ruler of three other church states. The Wittelsbachs' attitude to the aggressive re-establishment of Catholicism acted as a positive encouragement to those prince-bishops who were prepared to play their part in rolling back the tide of Protestantism inside their own borders. The Archbishopric of Salzburg, which formed a large wedge between Wittelsbach and Habsburg lands, was saved for the Church by such positive action, thus preserving the integrity of the potential heartland of the German Counter Reformation. In similar ways much of the north-west of Germany (especially those areas bordering the Rhine or the Spanish Netherlands), had come solidly into the Catholic camp by the end of the sixteenth century.

* The Habsburgs were less uniformly supportive of the Catholic revival. When Charles V abdicated in 1556 the younger branch of the family retained control of both the German lands and the title of Holy Roman Emperor, while the elder branch, in the person of Charles's son, Philip, was confirmed in possession of the major prize – Spain and its European and colonial empires. Whereas Philip's commitment to the Catholic cause – at least where it matched with his own interests – was strong, the Austrian Habsburgs (as members of the younger branch of the family were known) were variable in their attitudes. This variability was made more noticeable by the fact that the Austrian Habsburgs' land was not governed in a centralised manner. Not only did each province have its own customs and procedures in government, but it was likely to be ruled over by a separate member of the family. As a result, consistency in the treatment of religious issues was not normally apparent. This, of course, sometimes worked in the Catholics' favour, as when Maximilian II was Emperor and head of the family from 1564–76. If Maximilian, who was a Protestant in all but name, had exercised more direct power than he did, the Catholic Church would probably have lost its important Counter Reformation base in the south German lands. As it was, other members of the family were able to protect the interests of the Catholic cause while Maximilian was inactive in the face of spreading Protestantism.

The situation in the Habsburg territories remained inconclusive until the selection of Ferdinand of Styria as heir to the headship of the family in 1616. Ferdinand was strongly committed to the success of the political Counter Reformation, having been educated by Jesuits and having remained under their influence ever since. Although the story that he made a vow to the Pope that he would eradicate Protestantism in Germany is probably apocryphal, he is reliably reported as having expressed the view that 'I would rather rule a country ruined than a country damned'. His actions generally confirm this sentiment. As the direct ruler of the province of Styria from 1595, he was resolute in his determination to rid the territory of Protestants, all of whom were either made to recant or forced to emigrate. When he was elected King of Bohemia (traditionally a Habsburg fief) in 1617, King of Hungary in 1618 and Holy Roman Emperor (as Ferdinand II) in 1619, the scope for his activities was much extended.

    * It would, of course, be totally incorrect to suggest that the recovery in the Catholic position in Germany that had taken place by the early seventeenth century was exclusively due to the activities of the Wittelsbachs and the Habsburgs. In the highly complex political situation that existed both within the Empire and in European international affairs as a whole, there were many other factors of considerable significance. Among these the most important were the activities of the Jesuits (see pages 85–92), the soundly-based doctrinal position defined by the Council of Trent (see pages 50–57), and the influence exercised and the advice and moral support provided by the Popes of the time through their direct representatives, the Papal Nuncios, who were surprisingly often present when vital decisions were being made by the Catholic rulers of Germany. The Papacy operated a well co-ordinated programme of practical encouragement within the Empire from the 1570s onwards.

    However, the Catholic resurgence was not solely the result of the Catholics' own efforts. The weaknesses of their opponents also came to their assistance. The Protestants had lost their way politically after the Peace of Augsburg (1555) – at about the same time as the Church of Rome had completed its preparations to mount a counter-offensive against the heretics. Of course, even at the height of the Lutheran expansionary drive the princes leading the movement had rarely been prepared to sink differences of opinion or of interest in the pursuit of a common goal. Shrewd opponents had, therefore, always found it relatively simple to disrupt the fragile unity of the Lutheran camp, as Charles V had so successfully done in the 1540s.

    In the second half of the century the Protestants were in even greater disarray, when the complicating factor of Calvinism was added to the existing network of internal rivalries. It could even be argued with some justification that an analysis which treats the religious situation in Germany from the 1580s onwards as a two-way split between Catholics and Protestants is not particularly helpful. It is true that both the Lutherans and the Calvinists were Protestants, but there was almost as much that separated them as there was that united them. In doctrine, organisation and practices the Catholics and the Lutherans had more in common than the two Protestant groups, and most Lutheran rulers looked upon their Calvinist counterparts as political liabilities and potential disrupters of the public peace because of their extremism and their general reluctance to compromise. There was certainly no unity of purpose within the ranks of the Protestants. In addition, the potential of the Protestant group to resist encroachments from the Catholic camp was frequently reduced by the existence of struggles between Lutherans and Calvinists for the control of individual states. The Palatinate, Saxony and Brandenburg were all subject to such disruptions during the period of the initial Catholic counter-offensive.

In these circumstances it may appear surprising that the Catholic cause was not completely triumphant. However, the Protestants were not alone in their disunity. The political divisions among the Catholics were almost as marked. Besides the selfishness that almost always afflicts the relationships between virtually independent states co-operating together in a collective endeavour, there were additional complicating factors. Within the Empire, the fear of a possible Habsburg domination of Germany was often a more powerful emotion in the hearts of the Catholic princes than their dislike of Protestantism. There was, therefore, a tendency for the Habsburgs to find themselves deserted by their Catholic allies at just the moments when a clear-cut victory seemed to be at hand. The Wittelsbach dukes of Bavaria were the allies who most obviously acted in this way. They perpetually nursed the ambition to be recognised as the leaders of the Catholic cause within Germany, but they were never brave enough to launch their challenge in open opposition.

Of course, it was not only the Austrian Habsburgs who were suspect. Their Spanish cousins were also the subject of periodic suspicion within the German Catholic community. This was hardly surprising as Philip II and his successors were directly interested in maintaining influence along the western fringes of the Empire. If they were to achieve success in their much publicised aim of defeating the Dutch rebels in the Netherlands, they really needed a safe land route by which to transport troops and supplies from their bases in northern Italy to the scene of the fighting. This involved ensuring the existence of friendly governments throughout the Rhine valley, and implied a desire for domination.

The Catholic camp was further divided by the long-running power struggle between the Habsburgs and the kings of France. This struggle for dominance in western European affairs had been suspended for much of the second half of the sixteenth century while France had suffered the debilitating effects of weak government and periodic civil war, but by 1600 a somewhat restored France was ready to resume the challenge. True to its tradition of placing dynastic interests above considerations of religion, the French monarchy in the seventeenth century was prepared to act as a champion of the Protestant cause if by doing so it could injure its Habsburg rivals. The kings of France were also prepared to disrupt Catholic unity further by playing on papal fears of Habsburg dominance. In doing this the French were able to enlist the support of the Capuchins who were pleased to have ammunition with which to attack the position of their rivals, the Jesuits. The Jesuits' close identification with Habsburg interests was a cause of potential weakness for them in Rome.

This complicated network of interlinked rivalries and associations –

only some of which were a reflection of religious similarities and differences – was most apparent during the Thirty Years War (1618–48).

5 The Thirty Years War

In recent decades historians have been able to agree on very little about the Thirty Years War. All aspects of what was 50 years ago the commonly accepted view of the War have been challenged with varying degrees of success. Even its existence as a coherent episode has been thrown into doubt by those who claim that it was, in fact, a sequence of separate wars connected only by the geographical coincidence of being fought mainly within the Empire. A variation of the same argument is the challenge to the starting date of the War. Whereas it always used to be accepted that it began with the Bohemian Uprising of 1618, dates ranging from 1609 (the beginning of the dispute over the succession to Cleves-Jülich) to 1621 (the ending of the truce between Spain and the United Provinces) have been offered by a variety of authors as being more meaningful. As yet no consensus has emerged among historians.

There have been similar disagreements over the nature of the War. In the nineteenth century it was generally portrayed as the last of the great wars of religion, as the high point of the political Counter Reformation, and as the final struggle between Protestantism and Catholicism before the dawn of the age of doctrinal indifference. There are now no historians who would support this simplistic view, for all would agree that the War was made up of a series of overlapping strands, of which religion was but one. However, there is no agreement over the relative significance of the various strands – including the religious strand. Some commentators think that religion was no more than a smokescreen used by the participants in the War to hide their true motivation. They see religious goals as the publicly acceptable moral stance behind which selfish interests could shelter. Other writers maintain that religious aims were of major significance for some of the leading participants. As is normally the case where historians dispute heatedly and at length, there is actually insufficient evidence for a conclusive verdict to be reached. However, there are enough indicators in varying directions for each of the conflicting interpretations to be supported. Of course, this lack of conclusive evidence is hardly surprising. Given the ease with which human beings have always been able to delude themselves about their true motivation, let alone the efforts that leading politicians have traditionally made to mislead each other, and posterity, about their real intentions, it is not to be wondered at that historians have found it impossible to reach agreement on the complex web of motives directing the actions of rulers more than three and a half centuries ago.

The case for the Thirty Years War being regarded as a war of religion is simply stated. The War is traditionally thought to have begun in 1618 with the rebellion of the Protestant kingdom of Bohemia against its Catholic king, Ferdinand of Styria, heir-apparent of the Austrian Habsburgs, and the subsequent acceptance by the Calvinist Elector Palatine, Frederick, of the crown that the rebels had offered to him. Frederick was driven from Bohemia and the Palatinate after being defeated by the armies of the Catholic League (in reality the army of Maximilian of Bavaria) in 1620, and for the next twelve years until Frederick's death, the War was continued essentially because Ferdinand wished to destroy Protestantism throughout Germany, and because the supporters of the Protestant cause wished to restore Frederick to his inheritance of the Palatinate and refused to admit to defeat by the Catholics. Thereafter the War drifted on until both the Catholic and the Protestant sides recognised that they could gain no further advantage.

This interpretation is substantiated by the determined action taken by the Catholics, especially Ferdinand and Maximilian, to force all Protestants within the territories they controlled to return to the old faith. It is further strengthened by the facts that Ferdinand promulgated an Edict of Restitution when he was at the height of his military power in 1629, ordering all lands taken from the Church since the Peace of Augsburg in 1555 to be returned to it, and that when Gustavus Adolphus, King of Sweden, entered the War with dramatic effects in 1630, he did so as the avowed champion of the Protestant cause. Thus the religious motivation of the four leading characters of the first half of the War – the Emperor Ferdinand II, Maximilian of Bavaria, Frederick of the Palatinate and Gustavus Adolphus – seemed almost self-evident.

However, the classification of the Thirty Years War as a war of religion has been largely discredited. Throughout the War both the 'Protestant' and the 'Catholic' sides contained states of the opposite religious persuasion. From the outset few of the Protestant states of the Empire actively supported Frederick's cause, and some of them, such as the Elector of Saxony, actually fought on the Emperor's side. In addition, France, firmly a Catholic power by the 1620s, always acted with a friendly neutrality towards the Protestants, and was from 1630 their close ally and irreplaceable paymaster. By 1635 the labelling of the two sides as 'Protestant' and 'Catholic' had actually become meaningless. The War had become a struggle between France (allied to Sweden, the United Provinces and the Calvinist states in Germany) and the Habsburgs (supported by the Catholic and Lutheran states of the Empire).

In addition, even during the first half of the War, the motives behind the policies of the major participants were often selfish and political rather than altruistic and religious. Ferdinand II was guided in many of his decisions by two explicitly stated dynastic ambitions. He sought both to establish the Holy Roman Empire as an hereditary and autocratic monarchy for the House of Austria, and to secure his Spanish cousin's position in the Netherlands by crushing the Dutch revolt. Maximilian of Bavaria was driven by a determination to further his family's fortunes. He was promised, and received, Frederick's electoral rank in return for the assistance he gave Ferdinand in subduing Bohemia. This dynastic ambition frequently took precedence over his stated political objective of defending 'German liberties' from encroachment by the Emperor, which, in turn, often seemed to be more important to him than the furthering of the Catholic cause. Although Frederick of the Palatine was steadfast in his championing of the Protestants, he was very much under the influence of his Chancellor, Christian of Anhalt, who was an unscrupulous seeker of material gain for himself and his master. He was always able to persuade Frederick that selfish actions were really attempts to secure advantages for his religion. Gustavus Adolphus, although genuinely committed to the Protestant cause, was determined to exact a fair price for the assistance he gave to his German co-religionists, and his main purpose sometimes seemed to be the permanent establishment of Swedish control of the southern shore of the Baltic Sea.

6 Other Dimensions

From reading the earlier sections of this chapter the impression could reasonably have been gained that historians in the past believed that most of the political drive for the Catholic and Counter Reformations came from members of the Habsburg family. Although such a verdict has never been stated explicitly, this view emerges implicitly from a review of the way in which the topic has traditionally been presented by British and German historians. It emerges particularly strongly from the surveys of the personalities and events that have normally been given prominence in the standard narrative accounts. Yet a Habsburg-centred perception of the political dimension of the Catholic and Counter Reformations is now regarded as being misleading, as is an analysis of European international relations of the period 1550–1650 couched in terms of conflicting Catholic and Protestant blocs. Both contain elements of the truth but they are unsuitable ideas around which to form an understanding of the respective issues. Other 'organising ideas' need to be selected.

One major drawback of a Habsburg-centred analysis of the politics of the Catholic and Counter Reformations is that it ignores events in France. Yet the almost complete return of France to Catholic orthodoxy by 1700, after having been seriously in danger of abandoning allegiance to Rome towards the end of the sixteenth century, was one of the triumphs of the Catholic resurgence. In both qualitative and quantitative terms the saving of France for the Catholic Church was of major importance in the Counter Reformation.

So why is it given so little prominence by British and German historians?

This question has never been publicly researched, and thus there is little direct evidence available. But it is possible to surmise a number of probable causes from indirect evidence. Because the traditional perception of the Catholic and Counter Reformations has been that they centred on the Council of Trent and the events of the second half of the sixteenth century, the happenings of the seventeenth century have tended to be regarded as peripheral and of secondary importance. It is almost as if the extension of the Counter Reformation period to 1650 (as done by many 'authorities') has been an unwilling concession to the later period. Certainly, the treatment of seventeenth-century events (other than the Thirty Years War) has often been extremely scanty. As the reclamation of France in its entirety for the Catholic cause was not formalised until the revocation of the Edict of Nantes in 1685, it has often been considered to lie outside the chronological scope of the topic. The Counter Reformation in France has also been a 'misfit' in other ways. It was not inspired by the Papacy, being largely self-generated. Nor did it depend on the work of the Jesuits or the assistance of the Habsburgs. It was a mainly domestic matter, having few repercussions in international relations, and was in no meaningful sense a component part of a struggle between a Catholic and a Protestant bloc. As such it did not conform to the model according to which most historians have been working and has therefore been treated by them as being 'outside their territory'.

This tradition has been reinforced by the way in which European history has normally been studied in British schools and colleges. It is relatively rare to find the late sixteenth and the late seventeenth centuries being covered in the same course. Very frequently the end date of an 'Early Modern' course will be 'about 1600', 1610, 1648 or possibly 1660. The personal rule of Louis XIV in France (1661–1715) is almost always seen as belonging to a later period. Thus the Counter Reformation in France is effectively excluded from many students' consideration. However, if time allows, there is much to be said in favour of following up this theme in other books in this series. Doing so may directly assist the student in developing his or her own 'organising ideas' for the topic.

* The previously orthodox perception of the Counter Reformation as a struggle between the Catholics and the Protestants has resulted in a second distortion in the way in which the topic is often viewed. The emerging concept of the Catholic Reformation has been something of a corrective, but there is still some way to go. Counter Reformation studies have been tenaciously Euro-centred. This has been despite the fact that the vast majority of people who were recruited to the Catholic Church during the Counter Reformation period were non-Europeans, living mainly in the territories of the expanding Spanish empire in the

Americas. Yet the politics of their conversion has traditionally been of little interest to European historians, other than Spaniards. This situation has changed markedly in the recent past, but there remains considerable further work to be done in assimilating this perspective into the organising ideas by which the topic is studied. However, it seems safe to predict that in the medium term, future orthodox analyses of the Catholic and Counter Reformations will depend on approaches that are neither as Euro-centred nor as firmly rooted in the sixteenth century as they have been in the past. It seems that almost all aspects of the topic will undergo radical revision. In the meantime, it is for each reader of this book to develop his or her own ideas on the shape that a revised framework should take. It is in the formulation and justification of such ideas that much of the challenge (and reward) of studying history at an advanced level lies.

***Making notes on** 'The International Politics of the Catholic and Counter Reformations'*

You are likely to find this chapter the most difficult part of the book so far. This is because it attempts to make links with some of the other topics you will probably study during your course. But as you may not have covered all of these yet, some of the allusions made will probably leave you confused or unclear. Therefore, this chapter is likely to make most sense to you when you are nearing the end of your course. It is probably worth waiting until then to make your notes on it.

A second aim of the chapter will also partly explain its difficulty. In this chapter you are frequently invited to question historical interpretations and ideas on the way in which the topic should be studied. The intention is that you should begin to formulate opinions of your own. Obviously, this is a much more difficult task for most people than merely gaining an understanding of the views that are presented in a chapter. It requires much more thought on your part, and is likely to yield results that are tentative and vague. Readers who are looking for certainty will find this particularly unsettling. Yet it is an unavoidable component of studying history at this level.

The aims of the chapter might suggest the form in which your notes could best be made. Although the establishing of links and the formation of opinions takes place within your mind, the process is often assisted by the writing down of your ideas. This is the prime function of the notes you make on this chapter. You are not attempting to compile a record of what happened, as you have been in making notes on some of the earlier chapters. You are 'teazing' out sequences of thought of your own.

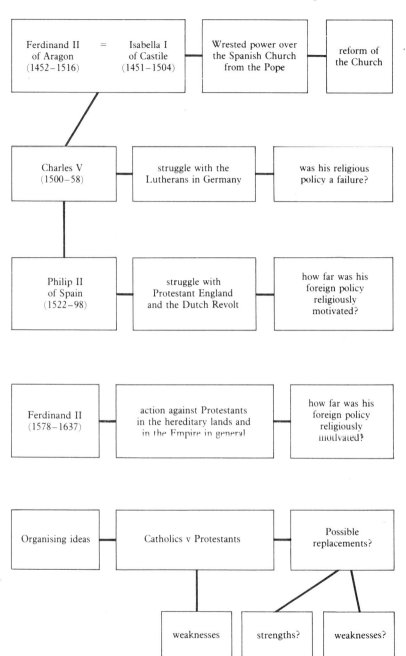

Summary – The International Politics of the Catholic and Counter Reformations

The simplest part of your task is to find answers to the question, 'What are the shortcomings of using the Catholic/Protestant split as the organising idea for a study of the international politics of the Catholic and Counter Reformations?' The more difficult part is to identify other potential organising ideas and to assess their relative strengths and weaknesses. Many readers will find that this is best done after extensive discussion with others.

Source-based questions on 'The International Politics of the Catholic and Counter Reformations'

1 Elizabeth I and the Catholics

Read the extracts from the Bull *Regnans in Excelsis* (page 122) and from the Act of Parliament of 1571 (page 123). Answer the following questions:

a) With what punishment did the Bull threaten those who continued to obey Elizabeth's orders? What was the significance of this?

b) What punishments did the Act of 1571 lay down for those who were convicted of publicising the Bull?

c) Many lay rulers (Protestant and Catholic) considered that Pius was exceeding his powers in the Bull. In what respect was it thought that he was doing this?

d) What justification was given in the Act for rejecting the Bull?

e) Was Parliament over-reacting to the Bull? Explain your answer in detail.

CHAPTER 8

Conclusion

Of all the study topics in early modern European history the Catholic and Counter Reformations is the one with the most uncertainty and the greatest number of unanswered questions. The debate among historians has been lively for several generations and is likely to remain so for a long time into the future. Why is this?

The foremost reason is the continuing problem over definitions. As the Catholic and Counter Reformations are concepts created by historians rather than by the people of the time, they are open to definition and re-definition in a wide variety of ways, with no one definition in a strong position to establish itself as 'correct'. In fact, 'correctness' has very little meaning in a context where no definition is likely to fit all the aspects of a phenomenon that covers millions of people over many lands and many decades (even several centuries), and where many definitions will cover enough of the facts to be plausible. So there are likely to be as many interesting new perceptions of the topic in the future as there have been in the past.

The choice of material presented in the previous chapters has provided one implied answer to the question 'What were the Catholic and Counter Reformations?' Even the choice of title for the book indicates acceptance of a particular interpretation. But there is no suggestion that the perceptions advanced here are in any absolute sense the correct ones. Of course, it all depends on your point of view. Other writers with other interests and other beliefs will justifiably construct other frameworks within which to give the topic meaning. It will be for each reader of each presentation to decide how far the formulation under consideration helps to illuminate the subject. Although some will undoubtedly shed more light than others, it is unlikely that any published work will be completely valueless. Therefore, it is important to resist the temptation to think that any one writer has a monopoly of the truth, just as it is vital to be vigilant in spotting any author who attempts to establish himself in this position.

Does this then mean that it is impossible to reach any conclusions on this topic? Fortunately not. But it does mean that care must be taken to define terms in every case. Once this has been done it is often possible to argue strongly and convincingly for a particular interpretation. For example, in this book it is assumed that the Catholic and Counter Reformations were mainly phenomena of the sixteenth and early seventeenth centuries. However, this is neither an explicit nor an implicit rejection of Delumeau's contention (see page 2) that events should be considered over a much-extended timescale. It is merely an acceptance that the traditional ways of perceiving the topic, which happen to coincide with the periods by which European history is most frequently studied at A-level, are also valid, and are ones that yield meaningful understandings. When this definition of timescale has been established, it is possible both to create other definitions and to discuss the major questions to which the topic gives rise.

The second important definition to establish is of the nature of the Catholic and Counter Reformations. Were they a self-generated spiritual revival or were they a response to the emergence of Protestantism (see page 4)? As should be very apparent by now, it is maintained throughout this book that they were both. Therefore, the question that immediately arises is, 'Which aspect was more important?' The current orthodoxy is quite clear on this. It is strongly and convincingly argued that had Protestantism never existed, something akin to the Catholic Reformation would still have taken place, whereas, had a spiritual revival not already been underway within the Church, it would not have been possible to mount an effective response to the challenges posed by Luther, Calvin and their followers. Thus it is clear that the spiritual revival within the Church is considered to be the more important. This should not, of course, be taken to imply that the reaction to Protestantism was not also very important. It was this that provided a focus for what might otherwise have been a diffuse movement lacking a sense of direction. It also imparted a much needed sense of urgency to the enterprise, especially by the Papacy in the mid-sixteenth century and by the Spanish and Austrian Habsburgs over several generations. It could even be argued that the Council of Trent, with its major achievements, is unlikely to have taken place without it.

The general questions that have most interested historians about the Catholic and Counter Reformations – apart from definitions and issues arising directly from them – have had to do with the *effects* of the movements. In particular, attention has been focused on the ways in which the Catholic Church changed as a result of them. 'What changed?', 'How far did things change?', 'Were the changes for the better?' and 'Did the changes strengthen or weaken the Church?' are typical of the questions that have been posed. In attempting to answer these questions it is, of course, vitally important to be clear about the timescale that is under consideration. As this book concentrates on the events that occurred in the sixteenth century, the phrase 'up to about 1600' should be taken as read throughout the discussion that follows.

Catholic historians, who unanimously view the sixteenth century as a period of progress for their Church, generally maintain that the change was from a weak and vulnerable Church to one that possessed such strength and resilience that it was able to meet the challenges posed by science, rationalism and materialism in the centuries ahead with success. They argue that it was the Catholic and Counter Reformations that ensured that Catholicism remained strong right up to the present day. What are considered to be the elements of this new strength? The emphasis has clearly been on institutional and doctrinal change. The reform of the Papacy that ended corruption and provided the Church with an effective and efficient centralised system of government has been seen as being particularly significant, as has the work of the Council of Trent in closely defining many of the beliefs that were to comprise orthodoxy for the future. The stress on the role of the bishop in ensuring the spiritual health of his diocese – by supervising the work of his parish priests and by making provision for the training of an adequate succession of high quality priests – has also been highlighted. The role of the Council of Trent is seen as fundamental in this process, although it is freely admitted that much good work had been undertaken by dedicated individuals in previous decades, and that the implementation of the Tridentine edicts on the role of bishops was delayed for more than a century in some parts of Europe.

However, not all commentators are convinced that the changes were totally for the better. It has been argued that some of the sixteenth-century developments set the Church off in directions that were not conducive to its long term health. Attention has been drawn to the way in which dogma was defined and policies were formulated in a narrow and conservative manner, which left very little room for manoeuvre in responding to the later explosive increase in biblical and scientific knowledge. As a result, the Church became entrenched in generally backward-looking attitudes and was for several centuries correctly perceived as being the enemy of most new ideas, be they religious, political, social, economic or cultural. In the twentieth century this fundamental conservatism has been especially apparent in the Church's official stances on the issues of social justice in the ex-colonial possessions (particularly in South and Central America), and women's rights (particularly over birth control, abortion and entry to the priesthood).

It has also been claimed that the way in which the distinction between the priesthood and the laity was drawn so firmly has also been unhelpful in the long term. The argument is that before the reforms took place most parish priests were clearly of the people. They were largely indistinguishable from their parishioners in that they dressed like them, shared the same entertainments as them, and often accepted the same family responsibilities as them. As a result of the reforms, especially the Tridentine Decrees, they were forced to separate themselves from their friends and neighbours. They were to dress differently, remain celibate, acquire an education and shun popular entertainments. In their exercise of their priestly function they were to distance themselves from their parishioners so that they could act as full intermediaries between God and Man, especially in the celebration of the sacraments. This trend, it has been argued, led to the Church being perceived by many people as largely irrelevant because its representatives ceased to share the cares and concerns of the man in the street, and were therefore relegated to the periphery – useful for officiating at the rights of passage such as baptism, marriage and burial, and for praying in times of crisis, but for little else. The Catholic priesthood has been unflatteringly compared with Protestant ministers who were in a strong position to maintain a close relationship of near equality with their flocks if they wished – as some did.

It has also been suggested that the growth of discipline within the Church was a mixed blessing, because of the way in which it was achieved. The contention is that the creation of a powerful centralised organisation, in which the emphasis for all those not at the top of the hierarchy was on unthinking obedience rather than on the exercise of reflective and responsible initiative, was too high a price to pay for an effective response to the challenge of Protestantism. It is maintained that the resulting conservative Italian domination of the Church left Catholicism ill-equipped to respond to the real needs of its followers outside of southern Europe. The assumption is that a less centralised Church would be more able to adapt to local circumstances.

Those historians who have argued for caution in accepting that the Catholic and Counter Reformations were totally to the benefit of the Catholic Church have provided a much needed corrective to the tendency to treat the achievements of the movements as an unqualified 'good thing'. However, care should be taken to identify the criteria used by such critics in making their judgements. It is clear that in many cases the adverse comments merely reflect the feeling that the post-Tridentine Catholic Church was not as the critics thought it should have been. Is such a criterion for judgement valid? Most historians would say 'no'. They would agree that the only justifiable criterion for judging whether the Catholic and Counter Reformations were to the benefit of the Catholic Church is the extent to which they assisted the Church in achieving its aims.

This presents the historian with difficulties, for nowhere are the aims of the Church spelled out. But some assumptions can be safely made. Given that the Catholic Church consistently claimed that it had a monopoly of religious truth, and that souls could only be saved through its ministrations, it is reasonable to assume that one of its foremost aims was to build up as large a membership as possible. Equally, it is safe to assume that the Church aimed to ensure that as many as possible of its members were saved, by making certain that they adopted the necessary practices. So it could justifiably be argued that anything that led to a net increase in Church membership or which resulted in a closer following of its practices was in its interests. Using such criteria it seems reasonable to argue that *on balance* the Catholic and Counter Reformations were to the benefit of the Catholic Church, even if it is very likely that they resulted in significant losses as well as major gains. But it should be remembered that such assessments are based on a subjective review of the evidence in general terms, and not on any careful statistical survey. In fact, even were such a survey to be carried out it would be very suspect in its results. There is clearly insufficient extant evidence for a reasonable degree of accuracy to be assured. Thus the assessment made is in no sense final. It is a matter of informed opinion, and as such is not to be unquestioningly accepted.

Similar statements could be made about any answers proposed to two of the other questions that are of prime interest to historians. Versions and variations of 'Were the Catholic and Counter Reformations successful?' and 'Why were the Catholic and Counter Reformations successful?' lie behind the explorations of many writers on this topic. Once again, the key process is the establishment of criteria – in this case for the assessment of success. And, as with the discussion on the 'extent of benefit', the only valid criteria would seem to relate to the achievement of aims. Assuming this to be so, it is reasonable to claim that a remarkable degree of success was achieved, given the constraints of the time. Not only was the disintegration of the Church in the face of expanding Protestantism halted, but areas that had been lost or stood in serious danger of being lost were also regained. In addition, the quality of pastoral care provided for ordinary Catholics throughout Europe was greatly (if patchily) improved. The Church was undoubtedly fulfilling its unwritten aims much more successfully in the early seventeenth century than it had been a century earlier.

Why was this? The component parts of the success are well understood – from the work of the Popes to that of the new religious orders (especially the Jesuits), the work of the Council of Trent, the endeavours of numerous local Church leaders, and the disunity and declining fervour of the Protestants. The difficulty is in apportioning relative importance to each of these components. Once again, the key issue is the determination of criteria – this time for measurement. On what basis should the relative significance of, say, the decrees of the Council of Trent and the work of the Jesuits be assessed? The only practical basis for assessment seems to be the extent to which the components under consideration actually resulted in the direct furthering of the Church's aims. This would seem to suggest that those 'at the front' (of whom the Jesuits were the most notable) deserve the highest ranking. But perhaps it is not quite as simple as that. It could be argued that all the components were equally important because had any one of them not existed success would have been in doubt. Here we enter the realms of the hypothetical – and, by definition, unprovable – because it is obviously not possible to be certain what would have been the outcome had something *not* happened. Perhaps it would be safer to restrict oneself to a judgement that some factors were directly responsible for the success of the Catholic and Counter Reformations while others were indirectly responsible. In effect this would be an assertion that it is only possible to compare like with like, and that the question cannot be answered directly. Such a verdict has much to commend it, for there is no shame in having to admit that in the study of history there is much that is not, and cannot now, be known. For some questions there are no 'correct' answers waiting to be found. It is this uncertainty, of course, that provides much of the continuing interest in the subject, and which makes it theoretically possible for any student to develop a valid and independent point of view.

Making notes on 'Conclusion'

As with the previous chapter, the difficulty of this chapter is very apparent. Its aim is to encourage you to think critically about the types of question historians ask and the ways in which they can be answered. As such, it could not be an 'easy read'. In fact, it needs to be studied closely and to be read paragraph by paragraph several times. It might even need to be noted paragraph by paragraph so that the steps in the argument are fully documented. But this should not be the end of the process. It is very unlikely that you will agree with all the points being made. It would be worth your while identifying in writing the arguments with which you disagree and the reasons for your disagreement. For most of you this will be an essential step in developing a coherent view of your own – a view that you will feel confident about presenting in the examination hall.

You might find that completing the following exercise will both clarify your thinking and provide you with notes that will be useful during revision.

1. Write each of these questions as a heading on a separate sheet of paper:

'What were the Catholic and Counter Reformations?'
'What were the results of the Catholic and Counter Reformations?'

2. Give as many 'one phrase' or 'one sentence' answers to each question as you can think of. Leave a three line gap between answers.
3. Using the notes you have made from the other chapters in this book, identify the evidence you would use to substantiate your answers.
4. Note down next to each of the answers you gave in step 2 the place where this evidence is to be found in your notes.
5. When you are practising making detailed essay plans, include the two questions listed in step 1 among those to be attempted.

Further Reading

There is a general lack of interesting or worthwhile books on the Catholic and Counter Reformations suitable for students studying at A-level. However, there are many books that would repay 'dipping' into in order to further your feel for the topic.

There are two general histories that are relatively accessible, although both are now somewhat dated.

A. G. Dickens, *The Counter Reformation* (Thames and Hudson, 1969)

This was written by an outstanding historian for the popular market. It is readable throughout and could serve well as a revision text. It contains more than a hundred contemporary illustrations.

Pierre Janelle, *The Catholic Reformation* (Collier-Macmillan, 1971)

This was used as a set book by the Open University in the 1970s. Although Janelle's judgements are consistently pro-Catholic, they are well informed and frequently challenging. It would be worthwhile reading one or two chapters.

Among the most enjoyable of books on the topic are those written by the Irish Jesuit, James Brodrick. His approach is reverential and uncritical but his works are sufficiently detailed to allow the reader to draw independent conclusions. The two volumes likely to be most readily available are:

J. Brodrick, *The Origins of the Jesuits* (Longman, 1940), and
J. Brodrick, *The Progress of the Jesuits* (Longman, 1946)

The standard academic works on the topic are worth looking at in order to acquire something more of the flavour of the subject, although none of them are immediately available in most public libraries. In particular, seize any opportunity you have to see either:

H. Jedin, *The Council of Trent* 2 volumes (Nelson, 1957 and 1961), or,
J. Delumeau, *Catholicism between Luther and Voltaire* (Burns and Oats, 1977)

One of John Bossy's books is both easy to read and widely available:

J. Bossy, *Christianity in the West, 1400–1700* (OUP, 1985)

This study surveys changes in religious beliefs and practices as experienced by ordinary people. Reading it will broaden your perception of the topic.

Two booklets have been produced explicitly for the sixth form and undergraduate markets. Unfortunately, neither of them goes far towards meeting the needs of the A-level student, although they both have much to offer to the undergraduate who already has a sound basic grasp of the subject. The ten page bibliography in the second booklet is particularly helpful to those exploring the topic at degree level. The two publications are:

M. Mullet, *The Counter-Reformation* (Methuen, 1984), and
N. S. Davidson, *The Counter-Reformation* (Blackwell, 1987)

Index